PI

LOCKED OUT

"A powerful account of courage, determination, and loss. The racially-motivated closure of the Prince Edward County public schools altered the trajectory of Alfred L. Cobbs's young life, forcing him to seek an education and future far from home. His moving personal story is continuing testimony to the extraordinary courage and determination exhibited by a generation of young Black students whose lives were forever changed by county authorities' embrace of massive resistance."

—Dr. Jill Ogline Titus, author of *Brown's Battleground: Students, Segregationists, and the Struggle for Justice in Prince Edward County, Virginia* and Associate Director, Civil War Institute, Gettysburg College

"*Locked Out* provides an inside look into one student's experiences in the years between segregated and integrated public education in Prince Edward County, Virginia—the years of NO public education. In Dr. Cobbs's case, denial of public education did not stymie his personal ambition. It furthered it. *Locked Out* is a must read and an undeniable inspiration."

—Lacy Ward Jr., Founding Director of the Robert Russa Moton Museum in Farmville, VA

LOCKED OUT

*Finding freedom and education
after Prince Edward County
closed its schools*

— a memoir —

By Alfred L. Cobbs, Ph.D.

Little Star ✳

Published by Little Star
Richmond, VA

This book is memoir. It reflects the author's current recollections of
experiences over time. Some names and characteristics have been changed,
some events have been compressed, and some dialogue has been created.

Library of Congress Control Number TXU 002 200 199
ISBN 978-1-7323915-9-8

Cover and interior design by Wendy Daniel.
Printed in the United States of America

For my brothers, Freddie and Samuel,
and the countless other students who were locked out of the
Prince Edward County public schools from 1959-64

CONTENTS

We have stories to tell that provide wisdom about the journey of life. What more have we to give to one another than our truth about our human adventure as honestly and as openly as we know how?

—*Rabbi Saul Rubin*

PREFACE

In the late 1950s and early '60s a popular TV series called *The Naked City* aired on ABC. It was a police drama set in New York City, and at the end of each episode the narrator's voice intoned an iconic line: "There are eight million stories in the naked city. This has been one of them." To be sure, there are not millions of stories growing out of the experiences of Black children who lived through the debacle caused by the closing of public schools in Prince Edward County, Virginia, in 1959—rather than desegregate as the Supreme Court ordered—but there are certainly hundreds of them. Mine is just one.

Friends, family members, and others have said to me over the years that I have a compelling story to tell and should write it down. However, at none of those times was I ready to tell my story about the impact the closing of schools in the county had on the trajectory of my life. It had to wait for its own time. As the writer of

Ecclesiastes 3:1 writes, "There is a time for everything and a season for every activity under heaven ... " When the time did come, the narration of that story in my head would not go away. Here I am reminded of Toni Morrison, who in discussing one of her novels said the story took hold of her and would not let go until she had written it down. While I certainly am not comparing my writing skills to those of the Nobel Prize winning author, I do identify with what she describes as the impulse to narrate a story that possesses one's psyche. So, I sat down and began writing. Sometimes I would wake up in the middle of the night, and a thought or idea would come to me. In order not to lose it, I would get up and jot it down on a scrap of paper and file it away. I would later find the right place for it.

Each of us has a story to tell regardless of the path of our lives, and it is shaped by our individual and collective experiences. In the pages that follow, I wish to trace my travels from the calm of childhood and adolescence growing up in Prince Edward County, Virginia, to the impending storm that followed the U.S. Supreme Court desegregation order of 1954, directing the county and four other litigants in the case to desegregate schools "with all deliberate speed." The storm would come in a form of defiance called "massive resistance," which was the Virginia General Assembly's response to the order. Following, in truncated form, is a discussion of the legal challenges and the history of the desegregation story in Prince Edward County and ultimately the closing of the public schools in the county in 1959 rather than desegregate them. While the case was working its way through the courts from 1959-64, my brothers, Samuel, Freddie, and I struggled to find a way to complete our secondary education. "Locked out" by the school closing but determined to succeed educationally and existentially, I ultimately found the study of the German language, literature, and culture a form of rescue. Dark days contained silver linings woven with threads of personal and communal tragedy, reconciliation and, finally, inner peace. This book reveals the finished tapestry crafted over more than fifty years.

Because this is a memoir, it reflects my recollections of experiences and people over time. I have in general included the actual names of individuals to whom I refer, because in many cases our paths have intersected, or we have encountered one another for a time, whether long or short. In other cases, the individuals have had positive, profound, and often lasting influences on my life. In passages in which I am critical of persons or my words might reflect negatively on them, I have omitted names.

*Amazing grace, how sweet the sound
That saved a wretch like me,
I once was lost, but now am found,
Was blind but now I see ...*

—Negro spiritual

*The real voyage of discovery consists not in seeking
New landscapes but in having new eyes.*

—Marcel Proust

ONE

HOPE AND INSPIRATION

My brother gunned the Dodge Fluid Drive to eighty-five. My other brother laid on the horn. We had never driven even a mile over the speed limit but were flying at twenty over that day trying to chase down the Greyhound bus that had left me at the "Colored Only" ticket window in Farmville, Virginia. I sat in back, on the lookout for police.

"Whites Only" ticket windows and discriminatory seating had been outlawed a few months earlier, but in Farmville, Virginia, the practice was alive and well. It wasn't just any old bus trip I was trying to take that day. I was on my way to Berea College in Kentucky, a place founded by abolitionists on principles of equality, and my brothers were determined to get me there. A series of miscalculations and discriminations challenged our simple goal of making the bus on time.

I can't explain why we arrived late at the Greyhound bus terminal in Farmville on that particular day, because Daddy had always taught us to arrive at the station early whenever we traveled. He felt strongly that if you arrived ahead of schedule for an appointment, you would never be late. He reasoned that we might have a flat tire or some other mechanical problem that would cause us to miss the bus or train, especially given the age and condition of our cars. Car trouble would be problematic for sure, as only a couple of busses and trains ran through our rural country town, even though it was the county seat. A rainstorm could also have delayed us. But we had no such problem that day, and as far as the weather was concerned, it was a beautiful sunny August day in Virginia.

Because of our late arrival, I missed the first leg of the twelve-hour bus trip that would take me from Farmville to Charleston, West Virginia, and from there to Lexington, Kentucky, and finally to Berea, Kentucky—my final destination. There I would begin my freshman year at Berea College, whose motto is "God has made of one blood all the peoples of the earth." It was this principle on which Berea defended its belief in interracial education, when it was founded in 1855 in a border state sympathetic to the Southern cause a few years before the outbreak of the Civil War.

The post-Reconstruction politics practiced by Whites in the South beginning in the 1870s, where the shadow of slavery loomed large, was a way of life. It was reality, despite the fact that ratification of the Thirteenth, Fourteenth, and Fifteenth Amendments to the U.S. Constitution between the years 1865-70 had freed the slaves, granted them citizenship, and guaranteed them voting rights.[1]

Once Blacks had been awarded full citizenship, they expected the promise of equal protection under the law. We now voted, won elected office, and served on juries. However, when federal troops were withdrawn from the South ten years after the beginning of the new experiment, power was returned to local White authorities. In the years following Reconstruction—the 1880s and 1890s—the White backlash was born, and the new White power structure began establishing laws to disenfranchise Blacks of their newly won rights. Blacks would begin to lose almost all of the gains they had made, and the denial of our rights and freedoms would be made legal by the enactment of a series of racist statutes, the "Jim Crow laws."[2] These laws reached into all aspects of society, and their purpose was to ensure the supremacy of the White race and to impede the progress of Blacks toward upward mobility and a better quality of life.

During the time when the independent Southern

states were enacting Jim Crow laws, the General Assembly of Louisiana passed in 1890 a statute called the *Separate Car Act*, the fact notwithstanding that sixteen of the Assembly's members were Black. It required all rail companies carrying passengers in Louisiana to provide "separate but equal" accommodations for White and Black passengers. A group of Black citizens joined by the East Louisiana Railroad Company challenged the law in court. The railroad company owners supported the lawsuit because of the additional costs the act would impose on them for more rail cars. To test the case, the group asked Homer Plessy, a man considered Black, even though, according to him, he was seven-eighths White and one eighth Black, to ride in a rail car reserved for Whites. Although he had a first-class ticket, he was asked to leave the car. He refused and was arrested for violating the act. He argued in court that his arrest violated the Thirteenth, Fourteenth, and Fifteenth Amendment rights guaranteed to him by the Constitution. After losing twice in lower courts, the case was sent to the Supreme Court which upheld the ruling and declared in 1896 the "separate but equal" doctrine as the law of the land. Despite the loss, members of the citizens' group asserted the justness of their cause: "*We as freemen still believe we are right and our case is sacred. ... In defending the cause of liberty, we met with defeat but not ignominy.*" Not until 1954 in its landmark *Brown v. Board of Education* decision did the Supreme Court overturn the Plessy v. Ferguson doctrine and declare it null and void.[3]

I believed that once onboard the bus that late August day, there would be no problem with discrimination in the seating arrangement because it had been outlawed a few months earlier. In fact, on September 22, 1961, the Interstate Commerce Commission outlawed discriminatory seating practices on interstate transportation and ordered the removal of "Whites Only" signs from interstate bus terminals by November of that same year. The catalyst for this change was the protest of the Freedom Riders, organized by James Farmer and the Congress of Racial Equality in May 1961. Its aim was to focus the nation's attention on the harsh reality of segregation and to put pressure on the federal government to enforce the existing law on interstate travel on public transportation.[4] They focused on two earlier cases—Morgan v. Virginia (1946)[5] and Boynton v. Virginia (1960),[6] in which the Supreme Court ruled in favor of the plaintiff. The court ruled that the Virginia state laws mandating segregation in waiting rooms, lunch counters, and restroom facilities, and seating accommodations on busses and trains for interstate passengers were unconstitutional.

In Farmville, Virginia, however, the issue of separate waiting rooms and ticket windows was another story. The Greyhound franchise there disregarded the Interstate Commerce Commission's ruling regarding the desegregation of interstate accommodations. Because of the disparity between the ruling and its application, I was denied service that day when I tried to buy a ticket at the "Whites Only" window. I was directed to the window marked "Colored Only." By the time I purchased my ticket, the bus was pulling out from the "Colored Only" waiting room and moving around to the one marked "Whites Only." Not seeing any White passengers, the bus driver drove off before I had a chance to board. What to do? To say I was outdone would be a gross understatement; indeed, my exasperation and frustration were at their limits.

My brothers, Samuel and Freddie, saved the day. Their lives, like mine, had been disrupted by the closing of schools in Prince Edward County by the Board of Supervisors. Rather than desegregate as the Supreme Court ordered in its Brown v. Board of Education ruling of 1954, Prince Edward County closed its public schools. My family, along with many of our Black friends and extended family members, had to pursue education in other counties or states. White families sent their children to "segregation academies," White only private schools recently spawned for the purpose of segregated education. Low income and impoverished families had no Plan B. With my younger brother Freddie, 17, driving my brother-in-law's 1950s Dodge at speeds of fifteen to twenty miles per hour above the posted speed limit of fifty-five, and my older brother Samuel, 20, waving a white handkerchief from the right front window of the car, we finally overtook the bus after a fifteen-mile chase. The Greyhound pulled to the side of the road, and I climbed in for the journey to the unknown world that was Berea College, nestled in the foothills of the Cumberland Mountains.

When I left the Greyhound station in Farmville that day, I had no idea what would become of me or where fate would lead. I know that I felt something like "a lost bird in the storm." The bus driver, having no inkling of the psychological and existential burdens I was carrying at the time, due to the political racism operative in my home county, chuckled, "You really wanted to catch this bus today!" He was right. I did really want to get away from the area, given the state of race relations there. Given my family's limited financial means, I had chosen Berea College not simply because of its commitment to interracial education, but because it did not charge tuition and had a work study program that helped students defray some of the cost associated with their tuition-free education. I knew it was economically right for me. But the whole experience would be filled with many challenges. My initial journey to Berea College in August 1962 was, as the old adage states, "the beginning of the first day of the rest of my life."

Each of the Prince Edward County children caught up in the struggle has a unique story to tell, each of which is a thread that makes up the tapestry of the combined experiences of the Black community after the tragedy that beset the county in 1959. The community had been educationally abandoned by the Board of Supervisors, and Blacks were powerless to do anything to change that. Mine is a story of loss, of floundering to find my way, and ultimately of triumph and of self-redemption. When I reflect back on the path of my life and career and gather the threads into a full tapestry, I now realize that while I was "blind and could not see," Providence was guiding my path. There was no way I could have known what I was doing when I decided to major in German at Berea College in 1963. Although my parents had allowed my siblings and me to decide what we wanted to study, they always insisted that we give it our best. But they, and even my siblings, wondered what on earth I would do with a degree in German. I certainly did not have an answer. With hindsight of more than fifty years, and given the wonderful things that have happened to me in that span, I know now that

I "was lost but now am found," and "Amazing Grace" became my theme song.

These insights came to me during my visit to Berea College, Kentucky, in June 2016, to attend my fiftieth Class Reunion, an event that I might have missed had I not been influenced by a fellow Berea classmate, George Giffin, with whom I had just reconnected. I knew him as one of the organizers of the Berea College delegation that participated in the Selma to Montgomery March in 1965, in which I participated. In fact, I was one of the students who carried the college banner for the delegation. I felt an overpowering need to participate in that march just as I did when I participated in the March on Washington in August 1963, along with my older brother, Samuel.

The events planned for the three-day weekend of the 1966 Class Reunion at Berea awakened in me much more than I ever could have imagined. The weekend culminated with a sermon given by Rev. Gail Bowman, at the time Director of the College's Willis Weatherford Religion Studies Center, at the Union Church on campus. Her sermon "Move, Immovable, Moved," based on Acts 17:28—"For in God we live and move and have our being."— spoke directly to me and revealed to me how God has moved in my life since I entered Berea College as a frightened, confused, and racially traumatized freshman in 1962. In response to Rev. Bowman's sermon and how it had helped me to "see" the role that Berea College had played in it, I wrote her the following:

My returning to Berea College for the fiftieth class reunion last weekend was an emotional and spiritual high for me. So when I came to Union Church on Sunday morning for service I was already on that plane. Your sermon and the music moved me even higher and onto an ethereal plane. They were most stimulating in every sense of the word! The sermon was an intellectual high for me and spoke directly to me in so many ways in terms of the movement of things in my life since the beginning of the Berea experience a bit more than fifty years ago, the movement of my own spirit, and the movement of God's spirit in my life. What I experienced was the meshing of the emotional, the spiritual, and intellectual in a way that I never could have imagined had I not attended the Reunion of the Class of 1966. "I was blind but now I see."

NOTES

Chapter One

[1] For specifics on each of the amendments and when each of the Southern states ratified them (the 13th amendment was at first rejected by Mississippi and not subsequently ratified); the 15th was at first rejected by Tennessee and not subsequently ratified), see U.S. Constitution, amendments 13, 14, and 15, http://www.constitutionus. com (accessed July 26, 2018).

[2] For a truncated discussion of the Jim Crow laws, see Constitutional Rights Foundation, "A Brief History of Jim Crow," 2018, https:// www.crf-usa.org.Black-history-month/a-brief-history-of-jim-crow (accessed July 26, 2018).

[3] In the petition Homer Plessy opposed the decision of the judge, the Honorable John H. Ferguson, and argued before the Louisiana Supreme Court that the 1896 law "violated the Equal Protection Clause of the Fourteenth Amendment ... as well as the Thirteenth Amendment, which banned slavery." Unfortunately Homer Plessy lost the case, and Plessy v. Ferguson became the law of the land until it was struck down by the Brown v. Board of Education ruling in 1954. For a short and concise treatment of the case, see: Gary W. Kinsey, "Plessy v. Ferguson," *Encyclopedia of Education Law*, Vol. 2, ed. Chas. J. Russo, Sherman Oaks, CA: Sage Publications, Inc., 2008, 644-45, http://link.galegroup.com/apps/doc/CX3073700004/ GVRL? (accessed May 11, 2018). See also "Plessy v. Ferguson," Oyez, https: //www.oyez.org/cases//1850-1900/163us537 (accessed July 26, 2018).

[4] The Freedom Riders played a decisive role in the decision of the Interstate Commerce Commission to outlaw in 1961 the discriminatory seating practices on interstate transportation. See Marion Smith Holmes, "The Freedom Riders, Then and Now," *Smithsonian Magazine*, Feb. 2009, https:www.smithsonianmag. com/history/the-freedom-riders-then-and-now-45351758. See also

Gavin Musynske and George Lakey, "Freedom Riders end racial segregation in Southern U.S. public transit, 1961," Swarthmore College Peace and Conflict Studies, Dec. 2009, edited with additional material Sept. 2011 (accessed July 30, 2018).

[5] The appellant in this case was Irene Morgan, who was traveling in 1944 with her baby by Greyhound bus from Gloucester County, Virginia, to Baltimore, Maryland, to reunite with her husband. During the trip she was arrested and convicted for not giving up her seat to a White man. Her sentence was appealed to the Virginia Supreme Court of Appeals which ruled against her. It was then appealed to the Supreme Court which ruled in her favor by striking down the Virginia law that mandated segregation in interstate passenger travel. Both appeals were done by attorney, Spottswood W. Robinson III, who would become famous for his role as one of the lead attorneys in the Brown v. Board landmark case. See Derek C. Catsam and Brendan Wolfe, "Morgan v. Virginia (1946)," *Encyclopedia Virginia*, Virginia Foundation for the Humanities, Oct. 20, 2014, https://www.encyclopediavirginia.org/Morgan v. Virginia (accessed July 26, 2018).

[6] This case involved the African American law student, Bruce Boynton, who was traveling in 1958 from Washington, DC to Montgomery, Alabama, via Trailways bus. At the 40-minute rest stop in Richmond, Virginia, he entered the section of the restaurant reserved for Whites and refused to move when ordered to do so. He was arrested and convicted, and the case finally made it to the Supreme Court, where it was argued by Thurgood Marshall. The higher Court ruled in Boynton's favor, using the Interstate Commerce Act of 1887, which bars all forms of segregation by race in any type of public transportation. See "Boynton v. Virginia: Summary & Significance," Study, 2003-2018, https://study.com/academy/lesson/boynton-v-virginia-summary-significance.html (accessed July 26, 2018).

Students carrying the banner of Berea College in the March from Selma to Montgomery on March 21, 1965. I am the individual standing behind the word "Blood."

(Personal Collection)

Childhood is a short season.

—*Helen Hays*

Childhood is a kingdom where nobody dies.

—*Edna St. Vincent Millay*

There is no land like the land of your childhood.

—*Michael Power*

TWO

CHILDHOOD AND ADOLESCENCE

When World War II came to an end in 1945, I had been in the world for one and a half years, having appeared on the scene in September 1943. It was only three years after President Roosevelt had signed the *Selective Training and Service Act*, which was the first conscription instituted in the United States. I was too young to understand war and politics, so I lived in ignorance and bliss, shielded from their influence on our lives. Because Daddy had not served in the military, he did not bring back from the European theater horror stories or those of bravery as many other fathers and grandfathers did. Daddy was 43 years of age when I was born. He was highly intelligent, healthy, able-bodied, and had excellent mechanical skills; he was a prime candidate for military service. However, he had gotten a deferment because of hardship—a classification for men whose induction would result in hardship to those who depended on them for support. And the family already had nine children. Also behind those decisions was always a local Selective Service Board comprised of White citizens. They were truly the ones who made the decisions of who would be spared military service and who would serve. Given services were racially segregated, it would seem reasonable to assume that my father had some allies among the Whites in the county.

My brothers, Samuel and Freddie, and I led rather sheltered lives in the late 1940s and early 1950s growing up on a tobacco farm in a rural community in the western part of Prince Edward County. Whites and Blacks had serious interactions only through work. After work and on weekends they went their separate ways. Socializing among Blacks and Whites basically did not happen. Even so, people got along rather well within those defined boundaries.

Our family lived in the second of two clapboard farmhouses built by our maternal grandfather, Nathaniel Hogue Booker. It was built on the exact spot where the first one burned to the ground in the '30s, constructed between the two original chimneys, which were also his handiwork.

My grandfather was known throughout the county for his chimneys constructed of fieldstone. The only cost related to the construction was the time expended to gather the stones and transport them by wagon to the building site. Both structures had been built on land—a hundred acres to be exact—that he had purchased a couple of decades after the end of the Civil War, no mean accomplishment for a Black man whose mother was descended from slaves. I, and other family members, have always wondered how he managed that. Did some benevolent White man, or one from whom he might have descended, lend him a substantial sum of money, give him a special break, or simply give him the land? He presumably made the purchase during the Reconstruction period; maybe he was able to see his way clear to manage the debt and pay it off on his own? We will probably never be able to answer that question.

The dwelling stood back several hundred feet from an unpaved two-lane country road. We lived in rustic splendor: water was drawn with a rope and bucket from an open pit well summer or winter, rain or shine. When the rope broke, some varmint got into the well, or the water table dropped, we experienced a household and barnyard water crisis, since we also had farm animals. I can recall on several occasions Uncle Thomas, Mama's oldest sister Aunt Daisy's husband, being let down into the well by rope and bucket to open the original water vein a bit or to find a newer or deeper one, which he always somehow managed to do. Once one of my older brothers, William, asked if he could try his hand at it, and Daddy and Uncle Thomas let him. That frightened me terribly for him. Uncle Thomas instructed him not to look up when he was down in the well or being drawn back to the surface. Why? Because to the person looking up, the opening at the surface would have appeared much smaller than it was, and the inexperienced well digger might have had a panic attack. Water for plumbing was out of the question since we had no indoor plumbing but an outhouse instead.

The seasons came and went, and we adjusted to their rhythm, submitting ourselves to nature and what each had to offer. Spring would often come in like a lion and leave like a lamb, as country folk used to say. March usually brought winds and snow flurries, drawing the comparison. The waning winter appearing as a sheep resisting fleecing. That was when farmers seeded their tobacco beds to give the seedlings time to germinate and grow large enough to be transplanted to the fields. When the beds were set out in February or March, they were covered with canvas to protect the tender seedlings until the earth warmed up, and covers were no longer needed. Then came April showers and May flowers. In the latter part of April, azaleas and crepe myrtle trees displayed their splendor, and by the end of May fruit trees were in full bloom, especially apple, sharing their beauty and fragrance. The daffodils smiled at the bright sunshine that caressed them with its warmth, and tulips bloomed in practically all the colors of the rainbow. In late May or early June, the tobacco seedlings, by then small plants, were set out in the fields to grow to maturity in the hope that with sufficient rain and the blessings of God the crop would yield a bountiful harvest.

Throughout the year, wonderful aromas filled the house as Mama made recipes she carried in her head. On occasion, the smell of pungent ginger in gingerbread made from local sorghum or from Karo syrup, bought at the country store, greeted us. She often made beef stew with onions and white potatoes for dinner, which smelled so good when it was cooking, we could hardly wait to eat it. We ate black-eyed peas and Great Northern white beans cooked with salt pork or ham hocks as our culinary staples during the winter months—our parents knowing that the legumes were a rich source of protein. And cooked with a small piece of meat, they offered healthy nourishment. It was wisdom passed down from one generation to the next in the community. My two sisters, Patsy and Alma, who were still at home didn't like the Great Northerns and refused to eat them. But Mama didn't cater to them. Instead, she would simply tell them they could go hungry or find themselves something else to eat, which they somehow managed to do. From time to time Mama made cornbread that melted in your mouth once it had been slathered with homemade butter. We were rich in ways that we only appreciated much later; we were "peasant kings" and didn't know it.

In due course summer followed spring, and the tobacco plants which had been set out in late May now spread their leaves over the furrows, reminiscent of a peacock or a turkey gobbler spreading its wings to reveal its fullness. That meant it was time for the backbreaking work of "suckering tobacco," i.e., removing the growth between the leaves and the stalk to prevent the leaves from falling off the plant prematurely. It was a weekly chore all summer long, and my brothers and I hated it. It strained the backs of all who labored, especially us kids. So it rankled us when on occasion an adult would say that we "did not have a back but a gristle instead." In this way they made light of our complaining because they understood that the work had to be done. At the end of summer, the tobacco had to be harvested and hung in barns to be fire cured, all of which was physically labor intensive. Many hands were needed for this task. There was also the harvesting of wheat and other grain crops. Since my brothers and I were in good physical condition, were good workers, and could do the work of an adult, we were often hired out to

White farmers because they needed extra field hands and we needed the cash. Whenever we helped White farmers with their crops, when it came to lunch, with a couple of exceptions, they ate with their families or alone in the dining room, while we were relegated to the back porch or the kitchen. Such were the ways of the Old South. However, a couple of the farmers defied this custom and ate with us. My brothers and I felt very good about this; we felt especially appreciated and valued. We were very pleased to encounter someone who had more liberal views on race relations than we were accustomed to; someone who did the right thing morally despite common practice in social mores in the community.

There were many things to be excited about in summer. While we loved school, it was nice to get a break from it. Relatives came to visit from northern New Jersey, New York City, Philadelphia, Baltimore, and Washington, and brought us stories from those parts of the country. Their stories and reports on their lives in the city enlarged our perspectives and gave us new and fresh images of urban life and of the world at large. One of the positive effects of their coming to visit was the meals that would be served when they were there. Mama didn't spare anything because you "put your best foot forward" and gave your best, when guests were there, even if they were family. We could count on country ham for breakfast, a luxury which we always got excited about, for it was generally off limits to us. The hams were used for quick income in the event that there was a financial emergency or the family needed cash for a special purpose. After all, in those days a country ham could fetch between forty and fifty dollars—no small sum at that time. At the other meals, fresh garden vegetables of all kinds were available in massive quantities. Every spot on the table was occupied by some dish. For example, there were fresh tomatoes, green onions, beets, cabbage, carrots, turnip greens, field peas, lima beans, string beans, and corn on the cob. So we could eat to our heart's content and "pig out" if we wanted to. There was plenty for everybody. There was no danger of obesity in our case because my brothers, Samuel and Freddie, and I did farm work equal to our abilities and worked alongside adult males. It was always high summer when the relatives came to visit, so the heat was often sweltering and sometimes almost unbearable. Naturally, there were always unwelcome visitors: house flies. Despite the fact that the house had screen doors and there were screens on the windows, the flies found their way into the dining room. There was feasting and fighting at the same time, for somebody had to shoo the flies away with a small bush and/or kill them with a fly swatter.

In the evening the visiting family members often

sat on the front porch and continued to describe their own lives and life in the city, while the cicadas graced us with their rhythmic buzzing symphony in the warm summer night air. The family members usually came in fine, late model cars and were dressed well. So we assumed that they were well off. In time we learned that they lived more or less from paycheck to paycheck, or from "hand-to-mouth" in current jargon. But what they had seemed like so much to us when compared to the meager financial resources and wardrobe of our immediate family. Aunt Darlie, Mama's youngest sister, was the most generous of them all; she bought groceries when she visited and always gave Mama a bit of money before she departed for home. When Mama said that she was working toward one day getting running water, indoor plumbing, and a screened-in back porch, Aunt Darlie contributed to each of the projects until they were realized. When they were completed anyone would have thought that Mama had traveled to the moon and back, she was so happy. I can still see her wide smiles and her tears of joy when the work was completed.

Near the end of summer when the stream of visitors from up North came to its end, my thoughts and those of my two brothers, Samuel and Freddie, turned to the beginning of the new school year, always an exciting time for us. In the early grades we attended a two-room schoolhouse where grades one and two were housed in one room, grades three and four in the other.

We were amazed at how each teacher managed to teach both grades in the same room and keep all of the students occupied. I especially remember my third and fourth-grade teacher, Mrs. Flossie Womack, for under her guidance I learned cursive writing and my multiplication tables. I still remember sounding like a broken record going around the house repeating them aloud like learning a song until I had mastered them, annoying my siblings and sometimes myself. She was the first teacher who gave me a sense of what can be accomplished under a gifted teacher with high expectations of her students. Years later when I became a teacher/professor, I came to realize that she was my first role model as an educator. It was tough love at its best.

The most inspiring teacher I had in high school before the Prince Edward County public schools were closed was Mr. James Stanton, who taught me biology in the 9th grade. I found him to be passionate about his subject and excellent at imparting it to his students. Under his tutelage, I became so excited about biology that I committed to memory all of the major phyla of the animal kingdom. The idea of me becoming a biologist was certainly within the realm of possibility. However, my trajectory as a student in the Prince Edward County public schools came to an abrupt end in 1959, when the

Board of Supervisors in the County closed the schools rather than desegregate them.

Because of the isolation of life in the country, my brothers and I found ways to amuse ourselves and to counteract the boredom that would inevitably set in from time to time. Besides, after school we had no substantial planned activities except the occasional sandlot baseball games we played with our cousins, and on Sundays, the walk through the woods to and from Sunday school. One of our pastimes in the summer was catching insects—wasps, bees, and hornets, for example, which we observed in captivity. The air holes in the top of the bottle notwithstanding, the insects usually succumbed in a couple of hours. As hard as we tried, we were rarely able to ever capture a monarch butterfly. As soon as we were within striking distance, it always eluded our grasp and would land on a lilac branch far above our reach. I often thought of how free and untouchable the butterfly was. What I had forgotten in that moment was that in its cocoon state it was in captivity. It was often my childhood wish to somehow escape my existential captivity and soar freely like the butterfly.

I remember very well how Samuel, Freddie, and I prepared our homework by lamplight until

the government agency, the Rural Electrification
Administration, brought electricity to the area in the
early 1950s. This transformation seemed like some
kind of a fairy tale to me and my brothers, especially
because it ushered the age of television into the
community. However, in those years no television
programs were broadcast into our house because we
could not afford a television set; the money had to be
used for more pressing needs. Daddy always said that
we were not "trying to keep up with other folks," as
country folk were fond of saying. This was a creed
that the farmers in the community swore by so that
they would not "lose the shirts on their backs," so to
speak, by indebting themselves too heavily. So during
the summer months we walked several miles one or
two nights a week to the Reid family, Mr. Sanford and
Miss Sue, our rural neighbors and family friends, to be
able to watch television. Among our favorite programs
were *"Cheyenne"* with Clint Walker, *"The Rifleman"*
with Chuck Conners, the *"Naked City"* with John
McIntire and James Franciscus, *"Ben Casey"* with
Sam Jaffe, *"Gunsmoke"* with Matt Dillon as the sheriff
and Amanda Blake as Miss Kitty, and *"Maverick"*
with James Arness. After watching television for a
couple of hours, homemade cake and ice cream were
served before the neighbor would drive us home. We
would repeat the ritual the next week. Years later,

my brothers and I could still recall the commercials for *Merita* and *Sunbeam* bread brought to us by the Kroger Store in Roanoke, Virginia, where one of the television broadcast stations was located. When party-line telephones came into the community in the early 1960s, our family was an immediate subscriber. Despite the fact that neighbors often interrupted or answered calls not intended for them, it was a positive addition to rural life in Southside Virginia. And in case of an emergency, the neighbors were more than happy to relinquish the line for anyone in need.

My daily chores, and those of my two brothers, were to gather up the eggs, milk the cow, feed the chickens and pigs, and water and feed the mules. In extra hot summers when the water table in the well receded, my older brother Samuel and I had to take the mules to a neighboring well for a drink. At the time the family owned two mules, the bay colored Molly and the rambunctious Mike, who had a grey coat. These animals belonged to the order of things in the family, so Mike's demise at some point during our upbringing was a somewhat traumatic one for us. One spring my brothers and I noticed that Mike had a visible growth in one of his nostrils. As it kept growing the mule became less and less energetic and lost much of his mischievousness. Daddy lanced the tumor a couple of times to no avail, for no blood came from it when he cut into it, and neither did it disappear or get smaller, and Mike never seemed to flinch when Daddy cut into it. By the end of summer, it was clear that he was suffering. Whether it was cancer or something else, we will never know, for we did not have the funds to have a vet deal with whatever it was. So, over our protests, Daddy took matters into his own hands. We watched as he wrestled with his decision to put Mike out of his misery. "Daddy, isn't there another way"?, we asked. His only reply was, "We can't afford a vet and he is of no use to us in this condition." It broke our hearts because we had grown up with Mike and regarded him practically as a member of the family, as children see things.

Samuel, Freddie, and I watched Daddy go about his daily chores and responsibilities as a farmer, always being positive despite the conditions and the possible threats to our livelihood that could come in the form of a tornado, wind, drought, or crop failure. He always said, "The Master will take care of us." To us, Daddy was a tiller of the soil who seemed to have a communion with nature that imbued him with a sense of inner peace and serenity matched by no one we knew. Although he had only completed the third grade, he had an intelligence and a wisdom that could not be acquired at any institution of higher learning and no degree could confer. He had what country folk called 'mother wit," i.e., real common sense, which he ironically told us was not at all common. I came to realize many years later just how wise he was. Many times in meetings with colleagues during my academic career as a professor, when someone would become "full of themselves" and let their ego emerge in full form, I was reminded of the words of my father, "When everybody around you loses their head and acts like a fool, don't forget who you are." It came in handy on many occasions at meetings when I would ask a simple question and remind my colleagues subtly that it was not about us the professors but about students. In most cases this brought reason back into the discussion or the deliberation.

A 1987 photo is of the farmhouse where I was born and lived from 1943-1959. It was built by my maternal grandfather.

(Personal Collection)

A photo of Five Forks school which I attended from grades one through four, taken in 1980. The school sat empty for many years after the closing of public schools in the county in 1959. It was later torn down.

(Personal Collection)

*I do not miss childhood, but I miss the way
I took pleasure in small things,
even as greater things crumbled.
I could not control the world I was in,
could not walk away from things or people
or moments that hurt,
but I took joy in the things that made me happy.*

—*English writer Neil Gaiman*
The Ocean at the End of the Lane

THREE

THE LOSS OF INNOCENCE

My brothers and I, and the entire community, experienced the mundane and repetitious activities and events of the late 1940s and the decade of the 1950s until this tranquility was shattered by tragedy. To borrow a phrase from the 19th century English novelist Charles Dickens, "It was the best of times and the worst of times." However, an incident took place at the beginning of the 1950s which shook the entire community to its very core; it was the train-bus accident of March 1951. It had been raining for several days off and on, but with the breaking of a new day, it appeared that the weather would be clearing up. As the other children in the family prepared for school, one of my older brothers, William, was "taking the day off from school" so that he could help with the shelling of corn which was an inside job that could be done rain or shine. Because our other older brother, Claude, had to take an important test on that day, Daddy understood that he had to let him go to school. However, on that day that would prove to be very fateful for the community, Claude went home with a friend and spent the night with him and his family. This fact alone removed him from the fateful event.

Although the rainstorm had intensified by mid-afternoon, the busses still loaded at their usual time, and the drivers cautiously left the loading zone. Because of the intensity of the rain, the bus driver for our route was acutely aware of the responsibility he had for the safety of his passengers. By the time the bus reached the railroad crossing about 12 miles from town, a heavy fog had set in, no doubt due to the rapid rise in temperature on that March afternoon. There were no railings at this crossing, a fact about which Mrs. Coleman, who lived in sight of the railroad crossing, had constantly complained to Norfolk and Western Railway Company to no avail. Under these inclement weather conditions, the student safety patrol officer was only able to discern an object in the foreground but not in the distance. Hearing and seeing nothing, he gave the okay for the bus to cross the tracks. In that fateful moment, the oncoming train struck the back end of the bus, spilling all of the passengers along the rail ties, killing at least five young people from the community. While this tragedy in the spring of 1951 shook the whole community to its core, the community would suffer a second tragedy in 1959 when the Board of Supervisors closed the public schools in the county rather than desegregate as ordered by the courts. This would ultimately have a greater and longer lasting impact on the larger community than the train-bus accident, as terrible as it was.

It was clear that the ugly event which fate played upon the community in March 1951 not only permanently changed the lives of the families of the mortally wounded children but that of the bus driver as well. He blamed himself personally for the deaths and could never get beyond it. In fact, after the tragedy he became a recluse and rarely ventured from his house—not as one who is agoraphobic, but as one who felt unwelcome among members of the community as a whole. As far as I know, the community never sent him those negative signs, but they were borne of his own emotions, despite the fact that friends and family continued to remind him that it was "an accident"; that he could not have known the tragedy that awaited them on that fateful day when the bus crossed the railroad track in the pouring rain and dense fog.

Folks who lived along the railway tracks and those who were driving in the vicinity heard the crash and the screaming of the victims as the train, moving at full speed, struck the bus. The impact moved the wreckage several hundred feet before the engineer could bring the train to a complete stop. By the time the authorities and the ambulances arrived, many of those who had witnessed the carnage were overcome with grief, were incredulous, and were helpless to do anything to alleviate the suffering.

Although the Black and White communities moved in separate circles in educational and social settings, in death they were for a time united and moved with one accord. The mourning touched all corners of the community, and on the day of the funeral every nook and cranny of the little country church was filled with mourners, both Black and White, cars lined the country road for several miles, and countless numbers of people who could not get into the church were there to witness, to feel anguish and pain, to share in the grief of the families who suffered individual loss, and to mourn as a single community now unified in a very special way.

My two brothers, Samuel and Freddie, and I were just young lads when the tragedy struck, so our knowledge of the event and the outpouring of grief expressed by the community at large came to us secondarily, especially since we did not attend the joint funerals. Years later, when visiting the local church cemetery, it struck us that all five of the children, four of them related to one another, were teenagers who had been struck down at an age when dreams and aspirations were being formed that would sadly never be fulfilled.

If the 1950s harbored loss and tragedy, it also contained moments and periods of excitement, joy, laughter, and fun. I can still laugh to myself at the degree of excitement that filled our hearts when the postman would deliver, as close to Christmas as was possible without bursting it wide open, sometimes even on Christmas eve, the "care package" sent from up North. It contained all kinds of goodies, among them both hard and soft candy, mixed nuts, and an Ann Parker fruit cake from the A&P store, a luxury that our family could never afford. The title of the autobiography by the Jewish comedian Sam Levinson, *Everything but Money*, describes our family's situation with regard to money, especially at Christmas, which always came shortly after the tax due date at the beginning of December. It was as if Santa Claus had never forgotten us and knew exactly what would make Christmas special for us. The benefactor was Mama's favorite sister from up North, Aunt Darlie, who had always adopted her sister's kids every Christmas, despite the fact that Daddy claimed that the nuts and the fruit cake had been sent to him by his favorite brother-in-law, Uncle Quinney. It is dubious if Daddy ever received anything from the package, even if he asked Mama to save some of it for him for later. Why? Because it all had a way of "disappearing on its own," so to speak, as if a vacuum cleaner had sucked up all traces of evidence.

Each year during the Christmas season Daddy would, at Mama's insistence, make one of his rare visits to see his Mother, Grandma Patsy. My brothers and I always wondered what had transpired between Daddy and his Mother during earlier years before we came on the scene that caused him to punctuate each of his visits with her with a span of several months, despite the fact that we lived only a few miles away from her. We never mustered the courage to ask him why. Of course, we were always happy to make the trek to see her because we could reckon with her telling "tall tales" about almost everybody in the neighborhood. She was a born storyteller—it was hard to separate fact from fiction, but it was entertainment that brought belly laughs and guffaws from us. Indeed, she always stretched the facts to the extent that she might have had the ability to become an author of short stories with a bit of coaxing and editorial assistance. Our reaction to her stories would bring forth from her the tongue in cheek reply, "I cla'r, I telling the truth," even when she knew that she was stretching it to its limits and beyond. Her knack for storytelling was also matched by her ability to make a liquid recipe of fermented dried fruit, the main ingredients being prunes/plums and peaches, which often caused men, both young and old, to lose their heads and sometimes their wits. Some even began to speak in tongues, but not the ones that the Good Book speaks of. I remember on one occasion when Daddy tested the recipe, he invented a new route home which he only abandoned when the smallest and youngest of us three boys, Freddie, began fretting. In that moment Daddy seemed to sober up. He turned the car around and headed home, missing the final turn and ending up stuck in the muddy road leading to the house of one of our neighbors. How we made it home, God only knows.

When Prohibition was lifted in 1933 with the ratification of the Twenty-First Amendment, taxes were levied on all alcohol production for public consumption. Since what Grandma Patsy was doing was illegal, she never paid what would have been her fair share of taxes. She was a survivor and had the task of taking care of three grandchildren single-handedly after her husband's death. They had taken the children in because their parents were divorced, their mother was trying to get back on her feet, and she lived out of town and could not afford to have them live with her. So for Grandma selling spirits illegally supplemented nicely the income she earned from raising and selling turkeys at Thanksgiving and Christmas and gave her the means necessary to take care of the grandchildren. The idea of her receiving Social Security benefits was out the question, since she had paid nothing in and was not entitled to monthly checks. I suspect that she probably defrauded the revenue agents out of more money per year than Daddy earned from the tobacco acreage that he cultivated as a sharecropper on a White man's farm. In fact, whenever the county sheriff was to pay a visit to the neighborhood checking on the illegal production of alcohol for public consumption, somebody would always tip her off, and her woodpile would temporarily double or triple in size. Until she was pretty sure that the "coast was clear," she refrained from dealing in her "illegal trade."

It was also in the 1950s when America lost its political innocence and the era of McCarthyism was upon us; it was the time of the Cold War after Khrushchev had come to power in the Soviet Union in 1953. At that time our oldest brother, Claude, enlisted in the Army in "defense of God and country," even if he and none of the rest of us knew quite what that meant. Only the grace of that same God spared him from being sent to Korea where countless lives on both sides were lost and "democracy was not won by the West." I remember well that a classmate of his who had been shipped off to Korea returned home with PTSD, which in the 1950s was labeled "shell shock." Although he did not go to Korea, my oldest brother was sent off to, what seemed to us, faraway lands within our country that we had heard of but thought we would never see— Kentucky and Texas. Although he was at Fort Knox, where the American gold reserves were held at the time, he never told us about Kentucky gold, and the stories from Texas seemed to have more to do with life and death than the ones from Kentucky. For example, he told us about the coral snake, which could kill a soldier in his sleeping bag in a matter of minutes by injecting him with a dose of deadly venom. I am not sure what he said about Texas weather, that is, the dust storms, the raging heat in summer or the tornados, or about its geography—the far distances, the wide plains, the sage brush or the flat country.

When our oldest brother returned home from the Southwest, he followed in the footsteps of our older sister, Mary Ruth, who had gone off to Virginia State College in Petersburg in 1950 to prepare herself for a career teaching little children how to read and write. How my brothers, Samuel and Freddie, and I wished that she had been our teacher because in our eyes no one could read stories to children like she read them to us. "Read that story again, sister?" "What did the first little pig do?" "Why did he do that?" "I like the way you read that story." I can hear us now as we begged her to continue what she had started.

In the decade that began with the Cold War and the loss of American innocence, we lost Mary Ruth, too. At the time of her death of a brain tumor at age 24, I experienced for the first time the bitterness of death personally with all of its mystery and power. I also saw how her death impacted my father, for I saw him cry for the first time with a sense of pain that came from very deep within. The strong and rugged image of a man who had been so stoic in my mind, had been very disciplined in everything he did, and who had very high expectations of his children, was now exhibiting vulnerability and human frailty. We were all sitting in the living room and all of a sudden Daddy picked up a green and pink paper mâché pig, which my sister had made as her project to be initiated into a AKA sorority while she was in college. As he took the pig into his hands and began to touch and stroke it, the tears came slowly, but then they seemed to have no end. He said nothing, and this moment of profound grief continued for what seemed to me like an eternity. It became clear to me at this point that Daddy was affected profoundly and touched very deeply by the loss of one of his children, who looked so much like him and had much of his intelligence. It was at this moment that I began to understand that the vicissitudes of life consist of a series of highs and lows, which none of us can escape. A few years later I not only understood them from a distance but would come to experience them personally and existentially.

You may encounter many defeats, but you must not be defeated. In fact, it may be necessary to encounter the defeats, so you can know who you are, what you can rise from, how you can still come out of it.

—Maya Angelou

The little reed, bending to the force of the wind, Soon stood upright again, when the storm was over.

—Aesop

FOUR

THE IMPENDING STORM

It was the end of summer, the last heat wave was upon us, and there were intermittent late afternoon thunderstorms, as was normal. However, late August was not only the time of the summer's slow waning, it was the time for spiritual revivals at the country churches and for school starting in a few weeks. Therefore, we were savoring the last days before the school term would begin. My brothers, Samuel and Freddie, and I were good students and loved going to school, and always looked forward to the opening day.

In late August and early September of that year, rumors of dark clouds appearing on the political horizon began to circulate. If we had been clairvoyant or had a crystal ball, we might have had some inkling of what was happening. However, our excitement and anticipation dampened in Summer 1959 when the announcer at the local radio station reported that the Prince Edward County Board of Supervisors had voted not to appropriate funding for the public schools in the county for the academic year 1959-60 rather than be forced by the liberal bureaucrats in Washington and the U.S. Supreme Court to desegregate the schools.

There was a "wait and see" attitude on the part of the Black citizens of the community. After all, they had very little political clout because they did not vote in sufficient numbers to turn the tide of post-Reconstruction politics in Virginia, whose capital, Richmond, had been the former capital of the Confederacy. When Daddy heard this, it seemed distant to him, as he and Mama had not been signatories of the 1951 petition to challenge the doctrine of "separate but equal" in the highest court in the land, the Supreme Court. The "separate but equal doctrine" had been sustained in the case of Plessy v. Ferguson in 1896 and had been the guiding legal principle governing the education of Blacks and Whites in the Southern States since Reconstruction.

The opening of school always coincided with the harvesting of tobacco in late August and early September. This was a labor-intensive activity. First the brittle, green plants had to be cut and left to wither in the sun. This was followed by placing them on sticks and then onto scaffolds. Finally, the tobacco was loaded onto wagons and transported to barns, where it was hung to dry before it would later be fire-cured. So that summer, when a Canadian television news crew came into the field where my two brothers and I were helping a neighbor with the harvest, and asked us what kind of impact the closing of our Prince Edward County schools would have on our lives, my brother Freddie spoke for the three of us when he said, "There would be a gap in our education." At that moment in time, we were naively optimistic that such a thing would likely never happen. But on the first day of school, the busses did not roll. We thought that it was a power play on the part of the Board of Supervisors in the county to flex their muscles, to show that they had the power to frustrate the efforts of the Supreme Court order to desegregate the schools in the county "with all deliberate speed." Being naïve and not "schooled" in the ways of Southern segregationists, my siblings and I assumed that the schools would re-open in a few days, or at least in a few weeks.

So we were happy to have a bit of an extended summer vacation. But that first day turned into days, the days into weeks, the weeks into months, and eventually the months into years—five years to be exact. It began to dawn on us that we had been confronted with the cruel reality that we and countless other Black students in the county had lost the opportunity for a public education, despite the fact that the Constitution of the Commonwealth of Virginia was supposed to guarantee a public education to all of its school-aged citizens, regardless of race or class.

In the face of this reality and the frustration of it all, Black parents and students struggled to figure out what to do or what course of action to take. During the first year some families sent their children to live with relatives in other states and localities, some relocated to other parts of the state, and some even moved out of state. In addition, there were enrichment programs and other limited interventions, such as teaching the basic learning skills, to try and offset some of the educational loss that the locked-out generation suffered. These initiatives were offered by grassroots organizations made up of several Prince Edward County Black women and former teachers. They were supported in their efforts by the American Friends Service Committee and the Virginia Teachers Association, the state Black teachers' organization. These measures made a difference for those fortunate enough to attend such programs. Eventually, some families inside and outside the state expressed their willingness to take a child into their homes to afford them an opportunity to get an education.

This became the solution for Samuel, Freddie, and me. In 1960, under the auspices of the Quaker organization, the American Friends Service Committee, a Black family in Moorestown, New Jersey, Mr. and Mrs. Clarence Baylor, took Samuel into their home. He lived with them for a year and a half, but after learning that they almost lost their home to foreclosure, his Quaker sponsor thought it best to move him out of the home. So during the last semester of his senior year, he was placed with four different families, two of them Quaker, one French Canadian, and one Black. All of the families had children. A family in Arlington, Virginia, Mr. and Mrs. Ernest Johnson, took Freddie into their home for two years from 1961-63, at which point he returned home to attend the Free Schools that were set up in the county in 1963. Freddie was among the first graduating class from the re-opened Prince Edward County public schools in 1964-65. I was fortunate enough to have been taken in for three years from 1959-62 by the family of the principal of East End High School in South Hill, Virginia, Mr. and Mrs. E.N. Taliaferro Sr. (I would like to note here that East End was also a segregated Southern high school which was the norm in the Commonwealth of Virginia at the time.) Due to the kindness and generosity of the principal's family, I returned to them each fall until I graduated in 1962. However, I always felt cheated that I did not have an opportunity to graduate from high school in Prince Edward County.

While I had a love of and some ability in math and had a fantastic teacher, Miss Vivian Goode Smith, it was at East End where I took two years of Latin with Miss Mary Tapp. Little did I know, but this would lay the foundation for studying and mastering the German language in college and eventually becoming a professor of German studies. There is a great irony in this fact: it was very unusual in the 1960s for a segregated rural high school in the South to offer Latin to Black students. Mr. Taliaferro, an enlightened educator, who had grown up on the South side of the segregated, former Confederate capital, Richmond, had received his bachelor's degree in math from Virginia Union University and had gone on to Columbia University Teachers College to earn a master's degree in mathematics education. He insisted that two years of Latin be offered in the curriculum, even if enrollment was always low. It is reasonable to assume that the Commonwealth of Virginia probably provided some financial assistance to Mr. Taliaferro to pursue a master's degree at Columbia rather than allowing him to attend the state's all-White flagship institution, the University of Virginia, where Blacks were not allowed to study. It was common practice for state legislatures in the South to resort to this technique if no Black institution of higher education in the state offered courses or a program in which Black applicants were interested in pursuing. The Virginia State Legislature passed such a law in the 1930s in support of this practice.[1]

Despite the anguish, uprootedness, and adversity that the closing of schools in my county caused, I still excelled at East End, becoming valedictorian. With diploma in hand, I matriculated to the integrated Berea College in Kentucky to study math. However, along the way I got derailed and pursued German studies instead. In this major I found excitement and eventually my calling in life. From the outset, I was fascinated with the grammar and structure of the language, for which the study of Latin had provided me the linguistic foundation. After Berea, I pursued a master's degree in German at the University of Missouri-Columbia and eventually earned a doctorate in German studies from the University of Cincinnati in 1974. After having received my degree, I was very fortunate to enjoy a long and distinguished career of 44 years teaching and researching German studies at several institutions: the

University of Cincinnati, the University of Virginia, and Wayne State University, where I spent the last 34 years of my career.

But not for the blessings of family, the generosity of others from outside the area, and our deep thirst for education, my brothers and I, whose lives were disrupted by the closing of public schools in Prince Edward County, might never have completed our formal education. Looking back over the impact that the closing of schools in Prince Edward County had on my life, I came to realize that I had been blessed by being able to turn a liability and a derailment into an asset. I found a profession that gave me joy, an income, and a good retirement. And my two siblings also found their way. Samuel became a middle school social studies and language arts teacher; Freddie became an engineer who worked for private industry. However, like all the others, I did not escape unscathed. The experience left its wounds, the pain of loss that all of us in the Black community suffered is permanent, and we are all diminished because of it. Yet, I still consider myself one of the fortunate ones. Others would be damaged, derailed, and disenfranchised for the rest of their lives and would never realize their God-given potential. They are the "lost generation" not only as far as a formal education is concerned, but also as fully contributing members of society. When I try to put myself in their shoes, I can only wish that fate had been as kind to those students as it has been to me.

NOTES

Chapter Four

[1] The law was enacted after Alice Jackson applied to the master's program in French at the University of Virginia, was denied admission, and challenged it. For details as to why the Virginia General Assembly passed this law in the 1930s, see Peter Wallenstein, "Desegregation in Higher Education in Virginia," *Encyclopedia Virginia*, Virginia Foundation for the Humanities, 7 April 2011, https://www.encyclopediavirginia.org/segregation_in_higher_education (accessed August 1, 2018).

The three brothers (Freddie, Alfred L., Samuel) affected by the school closing in the 1950s dressed in their Sunday best. This photo was taken a few years before the schools were closed.

(Personal Collection)

So long as any group is denied the fullest privilege of a citizen to share both in the making and the execution of the law which shapes its destiny ... that task is unfinished.

—Robert Russa Moton

We must achieve equal educational opportunities for all our children regardless of race.

—Attorney General Robert F. Kennedy

FIVE

THEY CLOSED OUR SCHOOLS

My brothers, Samuel and Freddie, and I were just kids when, on April 23, 1951, 16-year-old Barbara Rose Johns led a small group of students on a protest strike against what they viewed as inadequate educational facilities for Blacks in Prince Edward County Schools. I was only 7 years old, my younger brother Freddie was 5, and my older brother Samuel was nearly 9. We most certainly did not give much thought to the matter. Not in our wildest childhood dreams could we have imagined that the action on that fateful April day in Farmville, Virginia, would change forever the trajectory of our lives, that of our parents, of countless other Black students and their parents, and of Whites as well.

It is almost certain that when the core group of students from the Robert R. Moton High School staged their protest against the overcrowded classrooms and voiced their demand for a new high school equal to that provided for White students in the county, they could have had no idea what the impact of their protest would ultimately have on race relations in the county, the state, and the nation; that their action would ultimately lead to a landmark decision by the U.S. Supreme Court, the highest court in the land, to overturn the *Plessy v. Ferguson* decision of 1896, which upheld the doctrine of "separate but equal"; that their protest would have a lasting impact on the course of Civil Rights in America from the latter half of the 20th century to the present. They were a group of aggrieved students fed up with the "separate but equal" charade which had firmly ensconced itself in the American legal system, after the Supreme Court upheld *Plessy v. Ferguson* just three decades after the end of the Civil War.

The protestors highlighted the obvious differences between the facilities for Blacks as compared to Whites. The high school for Blacks had been built in 1939 to already overcrowded conditions. They became every more severe in the early 1940s, when private bus service was offered to Black students. The school was originally constructed for 180 students. By the time the walkout took place, the number had risen to more than 450. To alleviate overcrowding, the school board added three tar paper shacks to the grounds in 1948—barely 10 years after the high school opened. These structures were hastily and poorly built and looked more like chicken coops or barracks. The rooms were overheated in one spot and cold in another with the roofs springing leaks from time to time. The main building had no cafeteria, no gymnasium, and no science lab, and the auditorium fell short of seating the entire student body. The White Farmville High School had a gymnasium, a cafeteria, locker rooms, an infirmary, and an auditorium complete with stationery seats.[1]

When the superintendent of Prince Edward County public schools, Thomas J. McIlwaine, learned of the strike, he suggested that the School Board had been long aware of the inadequacy of the educational facilities for Blacks in the county. However, he saw no need for such a protest. According to him, a plan was "in the works" for a new county high school for Black students that would be the envy of what Whites were enjoying in their school at the time. Indeed, the superintendent was not amused by the action of the students, which he insisted was illegal: "The action of students at R.

R. Moton High School in remaining away from classes since Monday in the light of present information is considered a breach of discipline which should be met by measures on the part of the principal and faculty there."[2]

The superintendent's comments neither appeased nor deterred the student strikers. Barbara Johns had contacted the Virginia State office of the NAACP in Richmond to lodge the students' complaint against the Prince Edward County School Board. Curious as to how serious the protesters were, the NAACP dispatched one of its attorneys, Oliver W. Hill, to Farmville to meet with Barbara Johns's group. Convinced of their seriousness, the state office planned a meeting with the students and their parents, to be held at the First Baptist Church on Thursday, May 3, 1951. First Baptist was chosen because its pastor, the Reverend L. Francis Griffin Jr. was the sole clergy member in either the Black or the White community to respond positively to the student protest; he was also the county NAACP president. Rev. Griffin knew that this was a "hot button" issue that would exacerbate race relations in the county, but he made the moral choice in favor of the students.

As a result of the meeting, the NAACP drafted a list of the students' grievances with a request for their redress and passed them on to the Prince Edward

County Board of Supervisors, which was responsible for funding and maintaining the local schools. Not until this action was taken did the 450 students of the R. R. Moton High School return to the classroom. The students agreed to return to class on Monday, May 7, 1951, two weeks after walking out in protest of the unequal and inadequate facilities. In the Monday, May 7, 1951 edition, the *Farmville Herald* gave the following account of the meeting: "The return of students was announced last Thursday night at a public meeting of school patrons, held under the auspices of the National Association for the Advancement of Colored People at the First Baptist Church. The attorneys, Oliver W. Hill and Spottswood W. Robinson III, of Richmond, announced that the petition asking for the end of racial segregation in public secondary schools in Prince Edward County had been forwarded to the Prince Edward School Board."[3] As the NAACP saw it, there was no other way to stop this form of discrimination.

The petition on behalf of thirty-three Black students of Prince Edward County and their parents became the foundation for *Davis v. County School Board of Prince Edward County*. This became one of the five that constitute the *Brown v. Board of Education* litigation which resulted in the landmark lawsuit against the "separate but equal" doctrine which had been in force ever since the Supreme Court upheld the defendant in the case of *Plessy v. Ferguson*. The four other litigants were *Brown v. Board of Education* (Topeka, Kansas), *Briggs v. Elliott* (Clarendon County, South Carolina), *Bolling v. Sharpe* (Washington, DC), and *Belton v. Gebhart* and *Bulah v. Gebhart* (Delaware).

The petition, as summarized by the Associated Press and reprinted in the *Farmville Herald* on Tuesday, May 8, 1951, made the claim that educational opportunities offered to Blacks in the Commonwealth of Virginia were clearly unequal to those for Whites. Four fundamental points were cited in the petition[4]:

1. By enforcing section 140 of Virginia's Constitution (which says simply that White and Colored children shall not be taught in the same school) and section 12-221 of the Virginia code (which restates and amplifies the constitution provision) the county school board is denying Negroes, because of their race and color, educational facilities equal to those for Whites.

2. The separate secondary school facilities provided for Negroes are inferior in plant, equipment, curricula and other opportunities and advantages, to those provided for Whites.

3. So long as the board enforces the constitutional and code sections cited, it will be impossible for Negroes to obtain public secondary education equivalent to that possible for White persons.

4. Equality of facilities and opportunities can be reached only if no distinction is made on the basis of race or color.

Members of the Board of Supervisors were incredulous and faced with a dilemma. They did not need to stew for long because the governor, Thomas B. Stanley, had the Attorney General, J. Lindsey Almond Jr., file a legal brief with the Federal District Court in Richmond in defense of the status quo. The intervention on the part of the Commonwealth of Virginia was the first time that such an action had been taken by any state.

Shortly after the 1954 desegregation order was handed down by the Supreme Court, state government officials began searching for ways to fight it with as much resistance as possible. To this end, Governor Thomas B. Stanley appointed a commission made up of 32 state legislators, chaired by Senator Garland Gray (known as the Gray Commission), to draft the Commonwealth's response to the school desegregation order from the

Supreme Court. It recommended the suspension of the Virginia compulsory attendance law, encouraged local options, and established a voucher program, which would make it legally possible for White students to receive state funding to cover the cost of tuition at the newly established private segregated academies. All of these measures were approved by the state legislature.

At the urging of U.S. Senator Harry F. Byrd Jr., the governor and the General Assembly went well beyond the recommendations of the Gray Commission. In August 1956, Governor Stanley convened a special session of the legislature in which they enacted what came to be known as the doctrine of "massive resistance," a term coined by Senator Byrd. Its sole purpose was to delay as long as possible compliance with the court order in the hope of preventing desegregation. This doctrine led to the temporary closing of schools in Norfolk, Charlottesville, and Warren County (the City of Front Royal) in the fall of 1958 and part of 1959. Schools in Galax City were closed for a shorter period of time as school officials wrestled with a decision in view of the doctrine of "massive resistance." However, the Prince Edward County Board of Supervisors remained defiant and closed all public schools in 1959 rather than submit to the federal court order of 1954.[5] Public schools would remain closed until 1964, when they were forced to open their doors after the Court's affirmative ruling on a second lawsuit filed on behalf of Black students in 1961 as an amended complaint to the original case. In *Griffin v. County School Board of Prince Edward County*, the issue was whether the Commonwealth acted constitutionally in using public funds to support private, segregated schools while public schools were still closed.[6]

While *Brown v. Board of Education* was making its way through the courts in the early '50s, my brothers, Freddie and Samuel, and I had not given much thought to the political implications of the lawsuit and how it might impact the Prince Edward County community in general and our family in particular. To receive the news in the summer of 1959 that schools would not be opening in the fall left us at first incredulous and eventually stunned, once we realized that the announcement was indeed real. However, not in our wildest dreams did we ever entertain the idea that this closure would last for five long years.

Not only had the Virginia General Assembly allowed the Prince Edward County Board of Supervisors to close the local public school by de-funding them for the 1959-60 school year, they also suspended the law on compulsory school attendance for children until the age of 16 years. And they gave the local school jurisdictions the option to deal with the school issues as they saw fit. By 1959 the White business community in the county had founded a private segregated school—the Prince Edward Academy, which opened its doors in fall 1959. During its first year of operation it was supported completely by private contributions. However, in 1960, the Virginia General Assembly made it possible for White students in the county to attend the segregated private academy by providing a pathway for them to pay for the instruction. They adopted a new tuition grant program making every child, regardless of race, eligible for grants of $125 or $150 to attend a nonsectarian private school or a public school outside their locality, and also authorizing localities to provide their own grants. The Prince Edward Board of Supervisors then passed an ordinance providing additional grants of $100 each so that each child attending the Prince Edward School Foundation's schools received a combined total of $225 if in elementary school, or $250 if in high school. In the 1960-61 school year the major source of financial support for the Foundation was in the indirect form of these state and county tuition grants, paid to White children attending Foundation schools. At the same time, the County Board of Supervisors passed an ordinance allowing property tax credits up to 25% for contributions to any nonprofit, nonsectarian private school in the county.

While the machinations of the Virginia General Assembly and the Prince Edward County Board of Supervisors were favorable for many White students, the offering of state tuition grants to all students in the county without regard for race was really an empty gesture, at least as far as Black students and their parents were concerned. Given the fact that most of the Blacks in the county had limited incomes, they would not be able to pay the full cost of tuition demanded by the public schools in neighboring counties or elsewhere or in nonsectarian private schools. However, in August 1961, a federal court in Richmond ruled that the county could not use any public money to fund private education as long as public schools were closed.[7]

Black families in the county struggled to come to terms with the situation and try and figure out what to do about the formal education of their children. Those families who were able to do so moved away. Some sent their children to relatives in other school districts or other states. Others still found slots for their children in schools in neighboring counties, but these numbers were limited since these counties were in general not willing to take on the responsibility for the education of the Black students from Prince Edward County. A limited number of students were taken in by families and "adopted" so to speak.

During the first two years after the closing of the schools, several efforts were undertaken to place Black students in situations where they could further and/or complete their formal education. One of the initiatives of the first year of the school closing was an arrangement which Rev. Griffin, with the assistance of the minister from Beulah AME Church, Rev. A. I. Dunlap, made with Kittrell Junior College in North Carolina to enroll a number of sophomores, juniors, and seniors in the College's high school program. Sixty-three students participated in the program in the first year.[8] Beginning in 1960 and for the next three years, the Quaker organization, the American Friends Service Committee, through its Emergency Placement Project, set up shop in the county and sent 47 Black students to live with Black and White host families in ten communities in 10 states. These students were now able to attend school and many received their diplomas.[9]

For the majority of students who remained in the county from 1959-64 a series of efforts were undertaken to do as much as possible to further their education on a limited basis. Several Black women in the county, including former public-school teachers, began grassroots schools in their homes or churches. The state Black teachers' organization (the Virginia

Teachers Association), the American Friends Service Committee, and volunteer groups set up training centers and summer catch-up programs to give students limited instruction in reading and arithmetic in an attempt to offset some of the educational loss. They also focused on citizenship, Black history, and current events. However, none of these limited educational interventions were full-fledged schools because the Black community did not want to get into the private school business or jeopardize the NAACP suit. During the first two years they served 600-650 students.[10]

Ever since the County Board of Supervisors had closed the schools in 1959 rather than desegregate, the courts as well as lobbying groups such as the NAACP and the American Friends Service Committee had been working in an effort to get them reopened. As a result, in 1963, then Attorney General Robert Kennedy, at the urging of his brother, President John F. Kennedy, spearheaded a "Free Schools" program for the students of Prince Edward County. The schools would be funded by foundations, corporations, and thousands of individual donors. The National Education Association helped with teacher recruitment, and many of its chapters made financial and other contributions. The United States Commissioner of Education, Dr. Francis Keppel (former dean of the Harvard School of Education) and his staff played a major role in teacher recruitment and curriculum planning.[11]

When the Prince Edward Free Schools hired Dr. Neil Sullivan, an expert in non-graded education, in August 1963, he faced a daunting task and had only a month to accomplish it. William vanden Heuvel, a special assistant to Attorney General Robert F. Kennedy and the point person for the U. S. Department of Justice for the Free School Project, describes the enormity of the task with which Dr. Sullivan was faced. In his words, it was:

... a project that required over 100 teachers, none of whom had yet been hired, to work in buildings that were not yet available, a project that had to be funded privately and for which no money had yet been raised, a program that would be centered in a small rural county in Virginia where the White Establishment was so hostile to the very idea of desegregation that it challenged the President and the Supreme Court of the United States to force it to comply with the landmark decision of Brown vs. Board of Education.[12]

By the time the Free Schools program began in fall 1963, both my older brother Samuel and I had already received our high school diplomas: I from the segregated East End High School in South Hill, Virginia, and Samuel from the private Quaker high school, Moorestown Friends School in New Jersey. However, our youngest brother Freddie would spend his junior year as a student participant in this educational experiment known as the Prince Edward County Free Schools, which he found quite stimulating and satisfying. The next year (1964) the public schools in the County were re-opened and he was able to complete his final year of high school in Prince Edward County system and get his diploma. For him it was a form of closure to the whole ordeal which Samuel and I sadly would never have.

NOTES

Chapter Five

[1] For a description of the inadequacies of the Moton High School facilities for which the students led the school walkout on April 21, 1951, see the following sources: *Prince Edward County Heritage 1754-2008* (Waynesboro, NC: County Heritage, Inc., 2008), 4; Bob Smith, *They Closed Their Schools: Prince Edward County, Virginia, 1951-1964* (Chapel Hill: UNC Press, 1965), 14-15; Jill Ogline Titus, *Brown's Battleground: Students, Segregationists, & the Struggle for Justice in Prince Edward County, Virginia* (Chapel Hill: UNC Press, 2011), 2-4.

[2] "See the following article in the local paper, "Moton Students' Claims Unjustified Board Feels Now (Superintendent Says New School Site Being Sought)," *Farmville Herald*, Friday April 27, 1951, sec. A [Rpt. Wednesday, April 25, 2001, sec. C]

[3] For the local newspaper story about the Black community in Prince

Edward County voting to strike for the end to segregated schools, see "Students' Attorneys File Petition To End Segregation In Schools (R. R. Moton Pupils End 2-Week Strike)," *Farmville Herald*, Tuesday, May 8, 1951, sec. A [Rpt., Wednesday, May 9, 2001, sec. C].

[4] "Students' Attorneys File Petition To End Segregation In Schools" (R. R. Moton Pupils End 2-Week Strike)," sec. A.

[5] For two excellent truncated and highly readable articles on the Moton strike and the resistance of the Commonwealth and Prince Edward County to the Court's decision, see James H. Hershman Jr., "Massive Resistance," *Encyclopedia Virginia*, Virginia Foundation for the Humanities, 20 June 2011, https://www.encyclopediavirginia. org/ massive_resistance. Ronald L. Heinemann, "Moton Strike and Prince Edward School Closing," *Encyclopedia Virginia*, Virginia Foundation for the Humanities, 21 January 2014, https://www. encyclopediavirginia.org/moton_school_strike_and_prince_ edward_county_school_closings (accessed May 11, 2018).

[6] For a short description of the amended petition, see Vivian Hopp Gordon, "Griffin v. County School Board of Prince Edward County," *Encyclopedia of Education Law*, Vol. 1, ed. Chas. J. Russo (Sherman Oaks, CA: Sage Publishers, 2008) 408-09, http://link.galegroup. com/apps/doc/CX3073700004/GVRL? (accessed May 11, 2018).

[7] For accounts of state tuition vouchers to help fund the education of White students in the private Prince Edward Academy, see Chris Ford et al, "The Racist Origins of Private School Vouchers," Center for American Progress, 12 July 2017, https:www.americanprogress.org/ issues/ ... /racist-origins-of-private-school-vouchers (accessed May 11, 2018). See also "Tuition Grants," Television News of the Civil Rights Era 1950-1970 (2015), https://www2.vcdh.virginia. edu/civilrights. glossary/topics.html (accessed May 11, 2018). For documentation on the County adding an additional $100 to the State tuition grants of $125 for elementary school students and $150 for high school students, see "Supreme Court of the United States—Griffin v.

County School Board of Prince Edward County (Va.)," Exploring
Constitutional Law at the University of Missouri-Kansas City Law
School, edited by Doug Linder, (1995-2018), http//law2umkc.edu/
faculty/projects/trials/conlaw/griffinvprince.html (accessed May 16,
2018).

[8] For the story of the handful of students who attended Kittrell
Junior College in North Carolina in 1960, consult the following
sources: Smith, *They Closed Their Schools*, 170-71. The Moton
Museum website, www.motonmuseum.org/kittrell-junior-college-re-
union-the-ame-connection (accessed May 11, 2018).

[9] For information on the AFSC Project, see Betsy Brinson, "The AFSC
and School Desegregation," *Friends Journal*, January 24, 2012,
mlkcommission.dls.virginia.gov/AFSC_and_school_desegregation.
pdf (accessed May 11, 2018).

[10] To learn more details about the enrichment programs developed
for the Black students who remained in the county during the
school closing, see Katy June Friesen, "Massive Resistance in a
Small Town Before and After Brown in Prince Edward County,
Virginia," *Humanities: Magazine of the National Endowment for
the Humanities* 34.5, September/October 2013, https://www.neh.
gov/humanities/2013/septemberoctober/feature/massive-resistance-
in-a-small-town (accessed May 11, 2018).

[11] Truncated details about how the Free Schools became a reality are
given by then Attorney General of the United States in the introduction
to Dr. Sullivan's book. See, "Introduction," Neil Sullivan et al, *Bound
for Freedom: An Educator's Adventures in Prince Edward County,
Virginia* (Boston: Little, Brown and Company, 1965), xvii-xix.

[12] William vanden Heuvel, "Introduction," in a reprint of the book
by Sullivan et al, *Bound for Freedom* (Farmville: Briery Creek Press,
2009), xxii-xxiii.

The Moton High School auditorium in the early '50s. It is spartan when compared to the one for Whites.

(National Archives and Records Administration)

*The auditorium of the Farmville High School clearly reflects
that the conditions in the White schools were much better
than those in the Black ones.*

(National Archives and Records Administration)

There were three tar paper shacks built in the '40s to alleviate
the overcrowded conditions at the Black high school.
This is a picture of one in the early '50s.

(Richmond Times Dispatch)

Picture of a 9th grade English class meeting in one of the shacks. Note that the wood stove is standing in the middle of the room and none of the students is sitting near it.

(National Archives and Records Administration)

Success is measured not so much by the position that one has reached in life as by the obstacles which he has overcome while trying to succeed.

—*Booker T. Washington*

SIX

STRUGGLE FOR AN EDUCATION

At her funeral, my brother-in-law, Rev. James H. Franklin Jr., eulogized Mama, and chose as his subject, "Dealing with Darkness." He quoted the theologian Nels Ferré, who said, "It is better to light a candle than curse the darkness." He talked about how faith informs and guides the life of a Christian and how Mama used her faith in dealing with the "dark events" in her life and in that of her family—those things that caused much anguish, many sleepless nights, and probably quiet and unexpressed disagreements with Daddy.

When the public schools in Prince Edward County

were closed in 1959 rather than desegregate, Mama stepped bravely into the darkness, grasping a candle and extending it to her family, making the decision that the last of her three children would finish high school, whatever it took. We never knew how much discussion she and Daddy had about the whole situation. Daddy was the breadwinner in the family and as a farmer in his mature years was probably less sanguine about educational possibilities for us and held a more immediate and pragmatic perspective. He saw the leaving of home of his last boys as a threat to his ability to manage the farm chores, which were labor intense and required many hands, especially given that he was almost sixty and had already suffered a heart attack. Be that as it may, in the course of the next four years my two brothers, Samuel and Freddie, and I had secured places to continue our education because of Mama's persistence and her dream.

Mama had kept this dream alive because she had already seen seven of her ten children receive their high school diplomas and wanted to see all of us do so. Eventually eight of the ten of us would go on the receive college degrees. Only the two oldest, Grace and Ethel, did not have the opportunity to continue their education, but their high school diplomas made it possible for them to find good civil service jobs up

North.

In September 1959, as we were harvesting tobacco on Uncle Thomas Allen's farm, one of the retired home economics teachers from the local high school, Mrs. Minnie B. Miller, came to tell my father that the family of the principal of East End High School in Mecklenburg Country, Virginia, Mr. & Mrs. E. N. Taliaferro Sr., was willing to take a child from Prince Edward County into their home for the purpose of educating them. She indicated that the former art teacher at Robert R. Moton High School, Mrs. Vivian Ross, had told the principal about our large family and how serious we were about getting an education; that she had called Mrs. Miller and specifically mentioned the Cobbs family. Mrs. Miller had come to ask my father if he might send one of his children. Before he could respond, I "volunteered" myself, and so it happened. If I had given my father time to speak, I don't know what he might have said. In retrospect, more than fifty years later, to my way of thinking, the ideal way to have made the decision as to which of the three boys would go, would have been for my parents to deliberate about this and make a choice, or even have us boys do something as mundane as drawing straws. But the activities of the day and the gravity of the school crisis left no time or space for that kind of clear thinking and deliberation. I realize in retrospect that it was an act of self-preservation that I wanted to continue my education without interruption. At that moment, I did not give much thought to the fact that my two brothers were really "in the same boat."

To this day neither of my brothers has made any comment to me about this, and I still do not know what thoughts passed through their minds on that day. If there was any resentment on their part that I ended up losing only a few weeks out of school, while they lost much more time, they never showed it. At this point in time, I perhaps owe them if not an apology at least a debt of gratitude. I am particularly proud of them for not letting their school hiatus break their resolve to earn a high school diploma and even to go on to college and graduate. Many in their situation were not able to reach those milestones. Although I knew that I would be getting an education, I also knew at the time how I would miss spending the school year with them, my parents, and my friends. Instead I would be spending it with strangers with whom I had very little in common except that they were high school students like me.

Because Mrs. Miller had come with the offer from the principal's family during the tobacco harvesting season and the family car was not in the best shape, Daddy wondered out loud how he would get me to South Hill, Virginia. The upshot of the discussion between Daddy and Mrs. Miller was that she would drive me there. On the day of my departure, Mrs. Miller and Mrs. Victoria Brown, a retired elementary school teacher from another community, drove me to South Hill to begin my schooling at East End High School. I can well imagine that Daddy had mixed emotions as he saw me leave home. On the one hand, he needed his boys to help him with the harvesting of the crops. On the other, he must also have wanted his last three boys to get an education. But he never expressed to us his thoughts on the matter.

The family making the offer no doubt figured that they were committing themselves for a year; however, from the outset they left the possibility open that if the schools remained closed, I should contact them. Neither they nor I could know that this scourge would not end until 1964. The family allowed me to return for an additional two years, finish high school, and receive my diploma.

Those were some of the most challenging years of my life. I had entered puberty and had lost my support system, consisting of my family, especially my two brothers, and the friendships that I had made at school in Prince Edward County. Not only was all of that lost, but I had to find my way without overstepping my bounds. I had to adjust to life within the principal's family. He was my guardian and my principal. I had to get along with their only son who was three years my junior. If he ever resented my being there, he never expressed it, but only showed me kindness and generosity. I wonder to this day whether they asked Nelson if it would be okay with him. I know that the family had also kept a young girl of high school age once while their daughters, Cecilia and Brenda, were themselves attending high school.

Mr. Taliaferro, the principal, was a man of very high standards and served as an excellent role model for his son Nelson, me, and the other Black boys in the school. He was a strict disciplinarian and insisted that boys show respect and not act more grown than they were. If they were wearing a beard or a goatee when they came to see him, he would ask them to remove the "fuzz" from their chin or face before he would seriously engage with them. When I started growing a small goatee at the age of seventeen, he told me to "cut that fuzz off your chin." I told him what is referred to as "a little white lie" and said that my father forbade me to shave before I turned eighteen. He relented and no longer insisted. It felt good since I was able to control very little in my situation. As junior prom time approached, and having been elected class president, I wanted to have a date and participate in all of the festivities. I invited Doreatha

Bracey and she was excited about being my date. She expected me to attend an "after prom" breakfast. I was excited about the possibility, but upon asking Mr. Taliaferro if I might participate, he immediately nixed the idea. Doreatha told me that if I could not attend the breakfast, she would not be my date. I felt that I was in no position to challenge Mr. Taliaferro, which meant that I ultimately went to the prom without a date. This was quite an embarrassment for me, especially since I was class president. After all, I had been chosen for the position because I excelled academically and was respected by my peers.

My sense of indebtedness and gratitude to the principal and his family can never be repaid, for they gave me the opportunity to complete my formal education and build a foundation to attend college. I had no financial ability to repay them but did feel the need to do something for all they were doing for me. Upon arising on Saturday mornings, I would dust the hardwood floors and the bookshelves, and then I'd start the wash. Of course, their son and I were always expected to wash and dry the dishes after each meal. In spring I planted pansies along the front walkway and helped with the planting of the vegetable garden behind the house which the high school agriculture teacher, Mr. Ernest Morse, had prepared.

Upon meeting the principal, Mr. Taliaferro, for the first time, he asked me what my ambition was. Because I was good at math and did not want to see myself as an agriculture teacher or county agent, the role model for young Black men who grew up in the rural counties in the South, I told him that I had envisioned myself as a research mathematician. I was not sure what kind of profession that was, but it sounded good to me and was something different. At the time I entered East End High School I was a seventeen-year-old whose future was uncharted and unknown. It was my high school counselor, Mr. Howard E. Robinson Sr., who took me "under his wing" and befriended me, even giving me a job in his office. Then in my eleventh grade year, his wife, Mrs. Anna Robinson, became my homeroom teacher and in the twelfth grade my senior sponsor as well.

Despite my emotional immaturity, my insecurities, and my existential plight, I excelled academically at East End High School, where I completed the last three years of high school and received my diploma. Academics was an area in which I could shine and that would be my refuge. Because of my love for and ability in math, one of my best teachers who challenged me to the limits was Miss Vivian Goode Smith, who taught me geometry. I can still see her saying to the class, "Can't you see that it's 'side/angle/side'? What's so hard about that?" Miss Smith was brilliant and humorous, but as tough as nails. I loved geometry and excelled at it to such an extent that she suggested that I do a project on cycloids and submit it to the State High School Science and Math Conference at Hampton Institute (now University) in the spring of 1961. It was Miss Smith herself, who at her own expense, I suppose, drove several other student competitors and me to the conference. Such was the dedication of teachers at East End High School. Thanks to her, I won second prize for my project and would go off to Berea College, Kentucky, with the avowed intent of majoring in math.

Although I did not know it at the time, the other teacher who had a great impact on me, perhaps the greatest, was Miss Mary Tapp, my Latin teacher. At that time my head was full of math and I still had the illusion that I would one day become a research mathematician. But Latin would become the foundation for learning and excelling in German, and for my gaining very quickly an insight into how language works. Miss Tapp died prematurely of cancer, but I am so happy that she lived to see me earn a doctorate in German and go on to teach at the University of Virginia. The last time I saw her was about forty years ago when I attended one of the East End High School commemorations.

While I have talked about my pathway not being easy during those years when the public schools in Prince Edward County were closed, I am sure that my two brothers had their own emotional and existential challenges. After all, my older brother, Samuel, lost one year of school, and my younger brother, Freddie, two. Samuel was taken from the rural community of tobacco farmers in Southside Virginia by the American Friends Service Committee and placed with a family in the Philadelphia area. In reflecting on his feelings once the decision was made to go, he spoke of his mixed emotions in having to leave his younger brother Freddie, his parents, and his Moton friends. However, once he arrived in Moorestown, New Jersey, he was placed with a delightful Black couple without children, Mr. and Mrs. Clarence Baylor, whom he found to be both kind and hospitable. Mrs. Baylor was a local public-school teacher and her husband was a produce manager at a local Safeway store. They introduced him to gourmet meals and took him on trips to Atlantic City and New York City.

In Moorestown, Samuel was placed in the private Quaker high school, Moorestown Friends School, which certainly must have been a challenge to a young Black man from the rural South where the public schools had been segregated. Friends School was an expensive, upscale private high school for middle- and upper-class students. The student body was all White and Jewish until my brother became the first Black student to ever attend in its 175-year history. In one of the many conversations we have had about our experiences during those years, he stated that "it was cultural shock to walk into an all-White school;" that "it was a daunting and challenging experience." But Samuel indicated that first day jitters did not last long because the environment and atmosphere were very positive. The teachers and students were cordial from the outset, and he never encountered any signs of overt racism.

In addition to the educational challenges, I can imagine the personal ones and the social deprivation he must have experienced living and studying among Whites—a completely new experience for him. I remember him talking about an attractive Jewish girl whom he found interesting, but he dared not try and date her. In our segregated rural Southern community, we did not cross any racial boundary as far as the opposite sex was concerned; it was taboo. I can well identify with the intimidation and insecurity he must have felt. Like me, he, too, was going through his teenage years and experiencing growth pains.

Samuel succeeded in graduating from Moorestown Friends School and enrolled in Hampton Institute (now University), where he studied elementary education and received his degree in 1966. His education was financed by a Quaker group from the Philadelphia area. After graduation he joined the National Teachers Corp through which he earned a Master of Education degree from Indiana State University after two years of study and an internship in the Gary, Indiana public schools. For four years he worked in a federally funded early childhood education program at Hampton Institute, where he met his wife, Sadie Fulmore, an elementary school teacher from Lake City, South Carolina, and a Southerner like himself. He went on to have a thirty-one-year career as a successful elementary and middle school social studies and language arts teacher in the Hampton City Schools, from which he retired in 2001.

My youngest brother, Freddie, in my view, deserves more accolades than Samuel or I. Despite his having stayed out of school for two years, he went back and received his high school diploma, then went on to receive a college degree. Here is the story: A group of teachers from Arlington, Virginia, came to Prince Edward County in summer 1961 to participate in an enrichment program for the children of the county. Part of their outreach was to identify a small group of students for whom they would seek to find home placements so that they would be able to attend the Arlington County schools. They found several families who were willing to take one child each into their home, so my brother was placed in the home of Mr. & Mrs. Ernest Johnson, with whom he spent two years, completing the ninth and tenth grades. After this experience, when the Prince Edward Free Schools were established in 1963, he returned home where he was the youngest and only child left at home. Although he never said it, it must have been difficult for a teenager who had lived in the Washington, DC area for two years to return to and readjust to a rural environment in a country house with parents, with whom he had had little interaction for two years and who were now sixty three, Daddy, and sixty-one, Mama. I could also imagine that things might also have seemed a bit strange from the perspective of my parents, having gone from three boys to two in the house, then to one, then to none.

Freddie was two years older than many of his classmates, his peer group had been dispersed because of the school situation, and he had to find young people with whom he could interact outside of school, which placed him in many dangerous situations, such as riding in a car with a driver who drank too much and was driving too fast on a country road. In January 1967, during holiday break from his second year in college, Freddie was in a terrible car accident which injured him badly. He nearly died. He had a broken pelvis, a smashed cheekbone, and a broken tooth, among other injuries. More than fifty years later, he still has a limp as a result of the natural fusion of the hip and pelvic bone.

He made it through a couple of surgeries, but his survival was touch and go for several weeks following. The doctors told Mama and Daddy on the night of the accident that he had a fifty-fifty chance, and if he lived, he would never walk again. Following the surgeries and the extended hospital stay, he was delivered home to Mama and Daddy for rehabilitation and TLC. They both rose to the occasion, but it was Mama who had the bulk of the responsibility, to which she dedicated everything she had. Freddie talked about her cheerful attitude and kindness to him throughout his recovery period; he indicated that she never frowned. His description of her countenance suggests that there was something angelic about her, like one sees in faces of caregivers and hospice nurses, but unlike them, she was not counting on losing the battle with death but winning it. It was as if she had implored the gods and her God to give her the ability to deliver more and more care, or they had admonished her to do so. It was as if she were trying to heap onto her wounded son all of the TLC that she had not been able to give when he was away from home for two years, 1961-1963, his brother Samuel who had also been away for two years, 1960-1962, and his brother Alfred Leon who had been away for three years, 1959-1962. She gave him her all.

The young man, who as a child never departed without saying goodbye to Mama and waiting for her response, instructed his Yankee born and bred wife, Pattie, whom he married some years later, to take care of his mother, should she survive him on this earth. He met Pattie in Binghamton, New York, when he had a student internship with IBM Corporation in Endicott. After having married her, he moved her South where she worked for over thirty years at Nationwide Insurance Company, first as a secretary and later as a customer service representative. Freddie introduced her to his extended family into which she was accepted with open arms, taught her about Southern ways of living, introducing her to "soul food" and Southern cooking, like black-eyed peas with bacon grease. She adjusted well to most of it, but to this day he has not convinced her to eat sweet potato pie and chitterlings, although she has "graduated" to making the pies and at least cooking the chitterlings.

Freddie survived the accident, went on to earn his degree in electronics technology from Virginia State College (now University), has had a happy marriage of nearly fifty years, and a successful career as an engineer in private industry, first as an industrial engineer with General Electric Company and later as a manufacturing engineer for Stackpole Components.

While at Stackpole he was sent on several foreign assignments to share his expertise with workers in company subsidiaries around the world: to Mexico to train operators in assembling and testing switches for electrical appliances, to Haiti to train operators in assembling and testing keyboards for home computers, to China to train operators in the assembling and testing of switches. He remained with Stackpole Components until the company closed shop in the Raleigh, North Carolina area and moved their operations to Mexico.

While Freddie insists that he has never found his "calling" in life, this notion is refuted by the fact that he and his wife Pattie served as Scout leaders in the Occoneechee Council in the Raleigh area for thirty years. Freddie worked with Boy Scout troops both at Wake Chapel Baptist Church and Redeeming Love Baptist Church; Pattie served at both churches as Wolf Den Leader for second graders. During those years they worked with 555 boys, forty-six of whom became Eagle Scouts, the highest rank that a scout can achieve. During their many years working with the Scouts, they took numerous trips, visiting Annapolis, Asheville, Atlanta, Baltimore, Birmingham, Charleston, Charlotte, Chicago, Cleveland, Little Rock, Memphis, Montgomery, New York City, Norfolk, Philadelphia, Savannah, Selma, Tuskegee, and Washington, DC. All of the arrangements, including bus transportation, were made by Freddie. Most of the cost for the trips was defrayed by the money the pack raised from popcorn sales, an endeavor to which both Freddie and Pattie dedicated themselves wholeheartedly. In fact, for a number of years, their pack sold the most popcorn of any unit in their council, Black or White.

For their work with the Scouts over the years, Freddie and his wife Pattie both earned numerous awards from the Occoneechee Council Boy Scouts of America, from the lowest to the highest. They both received the District Award of Merit, the Scoutreach Spirit of Scouting Award, the Whitney M. Young Service Award, the Lifetime Achievement Award from the Neuse River District, and the Silver Bear Award, *the highest volunteer award given by the Council*. They also received a number of community service awards, among them the Social Action Award from the Phi Beta

Sigma Fraternity and the Wake Chapel Baptist Church Recognition Plaque.

But for the generosity of others from outside the area and our deep thirst for education in the face of challenging odds, my two brothers, Samuel and Freddie, and I might never have completed our formal schooling and been able to prepare ourselves for the successful careers that we enjoyed. It is with deep gratitude that we have always acknowledged this fact.

A visit with my East End High School mentors,
Mr. & Mrs. Howard E. Robinson Sr., at the home of their
son in Manassas, Virginia, in 2014.

(Personal Collection)

To assert the kinship of all people and to provide interracial education with a particular emphasis on understanding and equality among Blacks and Whites as a foundation for building community among all the peoples of the earth.

—*Great Commitment #5 of Berea College*

SEVEN

BEREA: RACE RELATIONS AND THE WIDE WORLD

As the Greyhound bus wound its way through the Allegheny and Appalachian sections of the mountains of West Virginia, I closed my eyes from time to time, took catnaps, and let my mind wander. Finally, I ate the chicken sandwich which I had packed for the journey. It was immensely satisfying to enjoy the last bit of Mama's cooking which I would not taste again until Christmas, when I would return home for the holidays. In between bites, my thoughts returned to the home front and the experiences of the last three years of my life—the lows and highs, the moments of joy and sadness. At the same time, I wondered what my future at Berea College would be like and hoped that it would be positive.

Somewhere during the journey through West Virginia, I began a conversation with a young Black woman who boarded the bus in Roanoke, Virginia. In the course of our conversation, I learned that she, too, was on her way to Berea College to begin her freshman year. This put me at ease, for then I knew there would be at least two Black students at Berea. Her name was Geneva Rachel Johnson, and she was from Staunton, Virginia. As future Berea College students we talked about our forthcoming adventure, our fears and concerns, but we also talked about our anticipation, our expectations, and our dreams.

When the bus finally arrived in Berea, Kentucky, after our overnight trip, we disembarked tired, sleep-deprived, and bleary-eyed. At the Carlton Restaurant, which also served as the bus station, I was received by Jerry Tramwell, one of the dorm monitors from Pearson Hall, where I would spend my freshman year. I was eager to meet my roommate and hoped that he would be White, since I had never had a social relationship with White people and wanted to begin that experience.

I did indeed get a White roommate, but the relationship was problematic from the outset. I came with my problems dealing with racial issues and self-image, and I found a roommate who had been socially isolated, having come from one of the narrow hollows of West Virginia. So I suspected from the outset that we might not have very much in common. Still I persisted in trying to develop a relationship with him. There was a problem though; his feet stank, and he had body odor, in part I suspect because he did not wash his limited wardrobe or his body frequently enough. To avoid this problem myself, I washed my body and my few pieces of clothing often. Not knowing quite how to navigate my situation, I turned to a couple of the fellow students on the third floor to seek their advice. They suggested that I go to the dormitory house mother. I went to Mrs. Pauck and she indicated that they could give my roommate some money to buy new socks and underwear and a couple of shirts. The male students at Berea usually wore blue jeans or khakis with a striped or plain colored shirt. However, my roommate bought two white shirts instead of striped or plain colored ones. I was thoroughly flabbergasted by his choice, because white shirts at that time needed special care to keep them white, and they had to be ironed. When I shared that news with Mrs. Pauck, she was disappointed and annoyed as well, and told me, "I wish that you had gone with him shopping."

I wanted to move out, as several of my fellow

students on the third floor of Pearson Hall advised me to do. But I did not want to give the impression that I thought I was better; I was not. I stayed hoping things would get better, but they did not, although we stayed cordial with one another until the end of that academic year. I wondered why fate had dealt me that "set of cards," given what I was already dealing with. If I had been more secure and had not been laboring under the race and self-image issues, I certainly would have acted on my gut instinct and asked for a new room assignment, which would have assured me a new roommate. When it was all said and done I suspect that fate dealt him a more cruel hand than it did me, for he never graduated from Berea College, as far as I know. After graduation I went on to earn master's and doctoral degrees in German and to have a satisfying career of forty-four years as a professor of German.

Over the course of my adult life I have developed lasting friendships with countless White people, but it certainly would have been nice to have developed a serious friendship with at least one White person during my first year at Berea. The possibility was certainly there my sophomore year, but it did not pan out. Upon returning to campus in August 1963, I learned that I had been assigned a White roommate, James Burge of Nicholasville, Kentucky. Room assignments were made on the basis of credit hours, and anyone who had gone to summer school was moved up in the "pecking order." James had been moved up on the list and arrived on campus at the end of that summer before I did and requested me as a roommate because he knew me reasonably well and wanted a Black roommate. That was fine, and we got along well, despite the fact that we did not have a lot in common. Even though I wanted to, it was hard to build bridges to him because he often went home on weekends, and in his sophomore year he dropped out of school and got married. After that we lost touch with each other.

Freshman Week activities featured a hayride, where the planning committee matched up a girl and a boy on a blind date. I was curious what they would do given the limited number of Black students in the freshman class. They took no chances and only matched Black females with Black males. I ended up with Jean Logan from North Carolina. No doubt Jean had thoughts similar to mine before the hayride took place. Once the activity began and we compared notes, we were not surprised at how it had all been organized to conform to expected social conventions. The hayride departed from the square in front of the Student Center building and ended up at Brush Forks, a picnic area not far from campus. The activities included a cookout and square dancing, if my memory serves me correctly. It was a subdued evening because at the time, we were all—White and Black students alike—feeling our way through the racial landscape of the South.

Part of the taboo of race in the South was a relationship between a Black man and a White woman. It should come as no surprise that if I admired a White female and wanted to befriend her or flirt with her a bit, I was afraid to go there. I remember in English composition class how well some of the female students wrote. I learned later that many of their high school teachers had studied English at Berea College. Their compositions were so good that the professor would select a couple of them to read aloud. While they were producing work of "A" caliber, I was struggling to write well enough for a "C." I remember particularly well one pretty blond girl from Virginia. She was as pretty as I would have imagined Helen of Troy to be and was ironically also named Helen, but I would never have dared reveal that to her or anyone else. However, more than fifty years later, on the occasion of the celebration of the fiftieth anniversary of our graduating from Berea in 1966, I shared that thought with her. We laughed about it. And she asked, "Am I still pretty?"

Berea not only introduced me to the problems and issues of American politics, but also to world politics because of the international students on campus, especially from Africa and the Middle East. There were a considerable number of international students from many countries. However, the ones who fascinated me most were from Africa—a continent of which I knew very little. I felt it was from those Africans themselves that I could learn the most—Salome David, Harry Mbui, Michael Ndungi from Kenya; Sydney and Nabilla Williams from Ghana; and four students from a small college in Rhodesia that had been modeled on Berea. Harry Mbui was my roommate during my junior year; he majored in economics and returned to his native country to apply what he had learned at Berea to make Kenya a better and more productive country. Salome and Michael also returned home to Kenya; Salome became the director of a school for girls; Michael worked in the field of agriculture. Sydney went home to Ghana to also work in agriculture. When these students were at Berea, many of the African nations were gaining independence from colonial rulers and declaring themselves to be free. Kenya, Britain's last East African Colony, declared its independence in 1963. I remember the Kenyan students carrying around black, red, and green flags or wearing those colors in solidarity with their fellow Kenyans. They talked with pride about their newly elected leader, Jumo Kenyatta, a moderate in the struggle for independence and former president of the Kenyan African Union. They also went around reciting the Key Swahili term, *"Uhuru,"* meaning "freedom," and taught it to those of us sympathetic to their cause. In sharing in their euphoria at what it meant to throw off a colonial power and become first-class citizens of the new nation, it did not occur to me at the time that in a country where my family had grown up and lived under the shadow of slavery since its introduction into the New World, I might never be a first-class citizen in America.

There were a number of students from Arab and Asian countries: Sami Daghir and Milhelm Farhat from Lebanon, Bashir Khalil from Jordan, Ahmed Baharistan and his sister Nayer from Iran, Esen K. Lowrie from Turkey, and Aida Demujian from Armenia via Egypt. It was from these and other Arab students that I learned the Arab perspective on the Palestinian question as a counterbalance to the Jewish one. The international students formed the Cosmopolitan Club, to which many American students also belonged, including me. They sponsored international programs and dinners, at which they served native food specialties. It was at these dinners where I had my first experience sampling international dishes and learning to appreciate them. An East African coconut chicken recipe stands out. It was a concoction in which chicken thighs were simmered in coconut curry sauce, to which ginger, garlic, crushed tomatoes, and fragrant spices were added. This was topped with crushed peanuts and served with basmati rice. The dessert that stands out was baklava, a Middle Eastern sweet pastry made of phyllo dough, filled with nuts, and drizzled with honey or syrup. Berea College was expanding my horizons in lots of ways.

My exposure to cultural and artistic experiences in Prince Edward County, and even in the segregated schools of Mecklenburg County, Virginia, where I spent the last three years of high school, was limited to what the schools and local churches had to offer. The Whites in those two counties were also limited in their exposure as well. And of course, the Whites and Blacks in Appalachia, from which Berea at the time drew ninety percent of its student body, also had limited exposure. Berea College offered us the world, so to speak. It was a world much larger than anything I had experienced up to that point. It was life changing to me and the others who made up the ten percent from outside the Appalachian area and I couldn't imagine what it meant to the ninety percent from within the area. We had two required chapel programs each week, one secular in nature, the other religious. The secular one was on Thursday afternoon during which time no classes were scheduled, the religious one was on Sunday evening. Because both forums were considered to be part of the liberal arts education of Berea, they were required of all students. Attendance slips for both services had to be signed and turned in to a chapel usher, a position which I held.

Speakers and performers for the secular chapel services came from a variety of backgrounds. I remember a visit by the Kentucky native and internationally famous mountain dulcimer player, who had reached the pinnacle of her career, Jean Ritchie; a visit by the well-known Hollywood actress, Agnes Moorhead, who performed scenes from Shakespeare.

The Louisville Symphony came to campus on a couple of occasions and played works that highlighted the sections of the symphony so that we could learn what instruments were played in each section. I remember at least three Thursday symposia which lasted all afternoon or longer: a mock Republican National Convention, a mock United Nations program, and an informative program on the Atlantic Community (a term first coined by the journalist, Walter Lippman, in 1943) and the formation of NATO in 1949. One of the speakers was the American pollster, Elmo Roper, who was the first to develop a scientific poll for political forecasting.

The Sunday night chapels featured a series of well-known speakers, some conservative or traditional, but some rather controversial. Among them was the author of *The Secular City*, Harvey Cox. In his book, Cox argued that the church is primarily a community of people of faith and action rather than an institution, and that God is just as present in the secular as in the spiritual realms of life. Another speaker, William Sloane Coffin, the chaplain at Yale University in the 1960s, was a longtime peace and antiwar activist. He was arrested as a Freedom Rider in 1961 and was an outspoken and vociferous critic of the Viet Nam War.

Whether students chose to attend a church service on Sunday morning at a local church was up to them individually, not required by the college. I attended Union Church, which was situated on campus but was not the "official" church of the college; Berea actually didn't have an official church because of its nonsectarian philosophy. My choice to attend Union Church was based on two things, the sermons of the Scottish minister, "Scotty" Cowan, as he was fondly called by all in the community, and the Pipe Organ, on which many Baroque pieces of church music from the seventeenth century were played. This was a totally new and uplifting experience. Scotty Cowan's sermons were filled with a mixture of scripture, social gospel and poetry. Delivered without notes and in his Scottish brogue, they were wonderfully insightful and uplifting, well worth the investment in time on Sunday morning. In the more than fifty years since leaving Berea, I have rarely heard sermons so inspiring and uplifting. Many of the organ pieces that Professor Donald Farley played at Union Church were by German Baroque organists such as Michael Praetorius (1571-1621), Heinrich Schütz (1585-1672), Dietrich Buxtehude (1637/39-1707), Georg Friedrich Handel (1685-1759), Georg Philipp Telemann (1687-1767), and Johann Sebastian Bach (1685-1750).

Because I attended Union Church regularly on Sunday mornings, I was approached about participating in the church's youth group, Youth for Christ. Membership in the group was small and could not hold a candle to the numbers that showed up for the Baptist Student Union group or the Wesleyan Foundation Youth group. Among the participants in the small group were Glenn and Susan, with whom I got along particularly well. We were not close friends and our relationship was limited to meetings and activities of the Youth for Christ group. This meant that our friendship was a cordial but superficial one. We never talked about personal issues, race relations or matters of the heart.

In the course of the year, Susan took a special interest in Glenn and decided to invite him and me home with her for a couple days over Spring Break. She must have reasoned that Glenn would be more likely to accept her invitation if I were to come along, since Glenn was rather shy in her presence. It was my understanding that we had all agreed to meet at the appointed time and place so that Susan's parents could pick us up and drive us to their Kentucky home, located a bit more than an hour from campus. Glenn was a "no show," which neither Susan nor I expected. I figured that I should bail out, too, whereupon Susan suggested that I could still come along if I wanted to. I decided to accept the invitation after all and view the experience as an adventure. In retrospect, I realize that I was naïve and should have backed out because the experience was from the outset a very awkward and uncomfortable one for me as a Black male having an overnight visit with a White family for the first time, despite Susan's sincere invitation. The family was cordial and hospitable towards me and I felt that there were no subliminal racial undertones from either the parents or Susan. Had that been the case, I am sure Susan would not have extended the invitation. I suspect that my visit with the family was probably the first and the last Black house guest they ever had.

Upon my arrival at the family home I was shown

to the guest bedroom. As soon as I sat down in the room, I wished a thousand times that I had said no to the invitation, because without Glenn as a buffer in this situation, I was at a loss as to how I would move forward. I wondered what each member of the family was thinking before I joined them for dinner. And I am sure they were wondering the same thing. At the table the conversation was awkward because we had difficulty finding common ground. We talked about where I was from and the fact that I grew up on a farm. I thought this would be a good ice breaker since Susan's father was a farmer and Susan and her mother were accustomed to life on the farm. However, Susan's mother was from upstate New York and had taken a job as an elementary school teacher in a rural Kentucky village and had married a local farmer. We talked a bit about Susan's and my experiences at Berea and about the work of Susan's mother as a teacher in a rural Kentucky school. But there were many awkward moments which found us all grappling for threads on which we could continue the construct a conversation. My emotions were very contorted and at times I didn't know what to think or feel. I felt like I was groping in the dark. It might have been less awkward had Glenn come along, for as a White person he certainly would have felt more at ease in the situation than I, and his presence would have increased my comfort level.

That night after going to bed I had trouble settling in, for thoughts about the evening kept flooding into my psyche. I sure I did not sleep a wink that first night. I asked God to watch over me and deliver me from this situation. To complicate my awkward and uncomfortable visit, there was a snowstorm, and the roads in rural Kentucky were impassable for a couple of days. In short, we were literally "snowed in." If my memory serves me correctly, I spent much of the next day in my room reading and trying to come to terms with the experience. I wondered why the distance between Whites and Blacks had to be the way it was? And why I had allowed myself to get into such a situation? As soon as the roads were passable again, I had Susan's father drive me to the nearest Greyhound station where I bought a ticket and returned to campus, having a new experience in race relations under my belt. I was happy to be out of that situation and it took me some time to process it all. The "race thing" was still unsettled for me and the experience with the Kentucky family did not make it any easier. It would be years before I could bridge the racial divide and view Whites as individuals to whom I felt equal. But Berea had given me a start on living the College's motto that "God has made of one blood all the peoples of the earth."

While there was racial harmony and tolerance on the campus in the 1960s, the same cannot be said about the town of Berea or other towns and villages in Kentucky. The only semblance of a restaurant in town to which Blacks and Whites could go together was the Coffee Cup. If they wanted to go out to eat together—if they had any extra money, which was seldom the case with Berea students—the only places they could go were on campus: Little Mama's, Gilbert's Place, and the Carlton, a grill that also served as the Greyhound bus station. The segregation of the races in restaurants was the order of the day all over Kentucky and all over the South. One of my White classmates, who was a basketball player, relayed to me more than fifty years later a story from the early 1960s about the experience of the Berea College basketball team who went to Pikeville College to play. Of course, there were a number of Black players on the Berea team. When the group stopped at a restaurant on the way, the coach was told by the owner that the White players could eat inside, but the Black ones had to eat outside. In an act of solidarity, Coach Wyatt in his wisdom said to the owner, "Then we will all eat outside." Such a stance was and is reflective of the Berea spirit in the face of racism.

*To offer a high quality liberal arts education
that engages students as they pursue their personal
academic and professional goals.*

—*Great Commitment #2 of Berea College*

EIGHT

BEREA: CULTURE, ACADEMICS, AND AMERICAN POLITICS

Having grown up in a segregated rural society in Southside Virginia, I went to Berea College culturally naïve and not particularly well informed or engaged as far as national and international issues were concerned. After all, I had struggled to complete my high school education during the closing of all public schools in Prince Edward County. In my senior year of high school, I even considered the possibility of volunteering for the Air Force rather than being drafted into the Army and sent as "cannon fodder" to Viet Nam. So I took the Air Force admissions test, did very well on it, and considered enlisting. But I wasn't keen on the military. When the recruiter informed me I would probably be sent either to Keesler AFB, Biloxi, Mississippi, or Lackland AFB, San Antonio, Texas, I thought long and hard about the hot weather in those areas as well as what I'd heard about racism in the deep South. I wondered whether it would be worse than what I had experienced in Virginia. I decided I would ask for a military deferment and try college instead. So in the spring of 1962, I applied to Berea College and was accepted.

Shortly upon arriving on the Berea campus as a freshman, the possibility of being drafted into the Army became very real to me, despite the fact that I had gotten a deferment. The issue was raised because of the Cuban missile crisis of 1962 and the failed Bay of Pigs invasion, which could have led to a confrontation, from which the Russians fortunately backed down. I remember all of the boys meeting in the basement of Pearson Hall with the dorm director, Dr. Charles Pauck, where we discussed the missile crisis, the possibility of war, and the future. The fear of what might happen was palpable in the room that evening. We shared our thoughts and feeling with one another. We wondered if the United States would be attacked by the Russians? Would we would have a future at Berea College?

In 1962 the nation still had a conscription system and due to the buildup of American troop strength during the Viet Nam War, the possibility of losing the deferment at any time was never far from my mind. After all, I was physically and mentally healthy and Black. Deferments were subject to the approval of local Selective Service Boards, local committees made up of White citizens *only*, chosen from the community. If deferments were granted, they were based on grade point average and progress toward the degree. While I was zealous in getting the required paperwork to the secretary of the Selective Service Board in Prince Edward County, Mrs. Nell Harris, I still stood in constant fear of being yanked from school to be sent to Viet Nam to fight in a war and possibly make the ultimate sacrifice for a conflict that I did not fully understand, and to which I was opposed at the time but dared not express openly.

My fellow students and I in Dana Men's Residence Hall could not avoid reading about Viet Nam and American sacrifices on a daily basis. The *Louisville Courier-Journal*, at the time one of America's better newspapers, brought us stories about young men our age who were exhibiting bravery in all kinds of ways, risking their lives, and dying for a cause which they also probably did not understand and for which many, if not most, had probably not willingly volunteered. I put the Vietnam War and the threat of being drafted on hold as I concentrated on being the best possible full-time student that I could be at Berea.

While the interactions and relationships with my fellow students (mostly White) on campus were so important for my social and psychological development, the required liberal arts course offerings were equally as important to my intellectual and cultural development. In the latter context the required sophomore humanities course comes to mind. The course was a two-semester sequence which was team-taught by specialists in music, art, and literature. The pedagogical approach was topical, and the course was divided into five major units: sentient man (man as a sensitive, conscious being), building man (man creative and constructive), contemplative man (man who questions and speculates), social man (man concerned with his fellow man), and worshipping man (man's reverence for a supreme being). All the works of music, art, and literature studied were chosen to fit under the umbrella of those five units.

The music section of the humanities sequence was particularly fulfilling, and it was the first class on Tuesday and Thursday mornings. Mrs. Margaret Allen, the instructor, would throw open wide the window, even in the winter, and declare how wonderful the music was that we were listening to. In that course, we learned the basics about monophonic and polyphonic music, about scales and melodies, about notes and metrics. And we each had to write a simple melody based on the music scale. We learned about the instrument groups in a symphony. But the component that imparted the most to me was the "music listening" aspect of the course. We listened to and learned how Bach put together his seventeenth century piece, *The Passion According to St. Matthew* (1727); how Beethoven structured his 5th Symphony (1808); how Brahms achieved what he did in his 3rd Symphony (1883); what twelve-tone music meant and how Hindemith incorporated it in his composition, *Matthias der Maler / Matthew the Painter* (1934). This experience gave me the basics for starting my own collection of classical music and for developing an interest in attending chamber and symphony concerts.

What I learned in the art section of the humanities course prepared me for visits to art museums, something I had not done until I went to Berea College. In the art section of the course, we learned the primary color chart and how mixing of two primary colors gives one the secondary ones; about the materials used for particular paintings, such as paper, cardboard, and canvas; about watercolor, egg tempura paint, and oil paint; and about linoleum prints and woodcuts. We were introduced to the periods in art history. And we focused particularly on several paintings, Picasso's Cubist piece, *Three Musicians* (1921), Duchamp's *Nude Descending the Staircase* #2 (1912), Albert Ryder's *Toilers of the Sea* (1880-85), and one of the Calder mobile sculptures (mid-twentieth century). In addition, we studied the architectural details of a Gothic cathedral using Chartres Cathedral in France (1194-1250) as the example.

In the literature portion we became familiar with terms that describe prose and drama, including genre, narrative form and style, dramatic form and structure, and figurative language. We also learned terms that describe prosody, which is to say poetic description and form, rhythm and rhyme scheme, meter, the acoustic sounds of poetry, and verse type. Among the works we read in the course were several tales in Chaucer's *Canterbury Tales* (1387), Homer's epic tale, *The Odyssey* (800 BC), Shakespeare's drama, *Hamlet* (1599-1601), William Henry Hudson's exotic romance novel set in South America, *Green Mansions* (1904), and Edith Wharton's prose set in New England, *Ethan Frome* (1911). In addition, we read a variety of poems, among them several sonnets from Shakespeare.

At Berea I was also exposed to the repertoire of American theater plays for the first time. Among them were Tennessee William's *The Glass Menagerie* (1944), a play set in St. Louis, which reflects the memory of a son who longs to escape from the stifling home environment with his mother who suffers from histrionic personality disorder, and his mentally fragile sister, both of whom he supports financially; Arthur Miller's *The Crucible* (1953), a partial dramatization and fictionalization of the Salem witch trials in Massachusetts in the late eighteenth century; William Gibson's, *The Miracle Worker* (1959), the story of Helen Keller's breakthrough in coming to terms with her deafness and blindness, and leading a productive life; Eugene O'Neal's *The Iceman Cometh* (1939), a play in which a salesman tries to convince his barfly buddies to abandon their pipe dreams; and finally, some non-Aristotelian or Brechtian epic theater.

At Berea I witnessed for the first time a public performance of Handel's wonderful oratorio, *Messiah* (1741), performed by the Oratorio Society, a combined college and community chorus, which dedicated the entire fall to practicing and learning the parts for the holiday performance. I made it a point to sing with the group during my senior year since only regular attendance, but no audition was required to participate. This experience gave me the confidence to sing in the chancel choir of my church, which I have now done for more than thirty-five years. My church choir has had a repertoire of classical choral works, anthems, spirituals, and hymns. There was the college's Country Dance Society that preserved and performed the folk dances that the colonists brought over from the British Isles to the Southern Highlands in the eighteenth and nineteenth centuries, among them the Morris dance from England. There was the Cinema Guild that raised funds to support the showing on international films in foreign languages with subtitles, something new and exciting for me.

For all of the challenging times, there were also times of joy and excitement. One event I remember particularly fondly from my sophomore year is the one and only camping trip I ever made. It was with my fellow students from the all-male ancient philosophy class that we took with dean of men, Dr. James Orwig. It was a wonderful class and the bonding in the group was excellent. While I was happy with the class and with my fellow students, I decided on that night of camping that such an adventure was not "my cup of tea." We camped on top of the "Pinnacle" in the mountains located in the College Forest. I remember that I did not sleep well; that the rock on which the sleeping bag rested seemed to get harder and harder throughout the night; that getting up during the night in the cold—I think the adventure was in October—was no fun.

I remember fondly the celebration of Mountain Day each fall, for which the college cancelled classes, so that the entire student body and faculty would be able to spend the day hiking or mountain climbing in the College Forest. The purpose of the activity was to contribute to the bonding of students and faculty outside the classroom. At lunch time, all met in the college's Indian Fort Amphitheatre. The facility was built in 1955 to stage the outdoor drama *Wilderness Road* by Paul Green. The drama was about Berea College, its founders, and the role they played in Appalachia and in the cause of abolition.

At the end of my four years at Berea, the threat of being drafted into the Army was very much still hanging like the sword of Damocles over my head and that of my fellow seniors. Despite the fact that I had been given a deferment in each of the four years at Berea, I feared that upon graduation I would be given A-1 status, which was assigned to those ready to be drafted or who voluntarily chose to enlist. This was shown clearly to me when the local Selective Service Board in Madison County, Kentucky, in which Berea College was located, ordered me to show up at the Induction Center in

Louisville six weeks after having had an appendectomy with complications, and from which I was still wearing a draining tube. The order was given despite the fact that my surgeon recommended I not be required to show up for the physical exam. After all of the drama, I was given a medical deferment.

If fate had not intervened in several ways, I might have gone to Viet Nam and returned badly wounded or in a wooden box. The fate to which I refer was an acute case of appendicitis that was at first misdiagnosed, and as the result of which I could have died. Because my appendix was in retrocecal position—the relation existing between the position of the appendix and the acute inflammation was atypical—the signs and symptoms were also atypical. While ultrasound might have identified the problem immediately, this diagnostic tool was not in wide use at most hospitals, and especially not at a small local hospital like the one in Berea. And the CAT scan would not be invented for another seven years. This meant that the symptoms—vomiting and pain in the lower abdomen—were those that could also have indicated gallbladder or liver problems, kidney or unitary tract problems, or even a stomach virus. The attending physician and director of the Berea College Student Health Services, Dr. David Blackburn, diagnosed my case as a stomach virus and sent me home with orders to stay in bed and drink plenty of fluids. I was to come back in a day or two if things did not improve. Overnight the vomiting continued intermittently and the pain increased. Suffering a bit now, slowly and laboriously, I made my way back to the Student Health Service. This time I was treated by Dr. Dorothy Gates, the second of the two physicians working in the clinic. Having been a missionary doctor in India, based on the white blood count and the nature and location of the pain, she correctly diagnosed my case as one of acute appendicitis which demanded immediate surgery.

This was a dilemma for the Berea College Hospital; on that day no surgeon was in to perform the surgery. I would need to be transferred to the nearest hospital where there was an attending surgeon. Because I did not have student health insurance which the college did not require at the time, and because the meager earnings of my father did not provide enough funds to pay the bills and cover insurance, the cost of ambulance transport from the Berea College Hospital to the Patty M. Clay Infirmary in the neighboring town of Richmond was an issue. So the director of the Berea College Student Health Services asked who might drive me to the hospital in Richmond. It was the good will of my German professors, Mr. Kris and Mrs. Amanda Kogerma, who took on the task. Out of concern for my health, one of the nurses from the hospital, Mrs. Powell, whom I will never forget, got permission from her supervisor to take time off to accompany me in the van to the Patty Clay Infirmary. The three of them stayed with me during surgery and during the recovery period because I was still a very sick young man. The surgery was done just six weeks before graduation. I was still recovering from it during that time but had to catch up on my schoolwork in time to graduate. Somehow, I made it.

Instead of being drafted into the military, I chose to enroll in the Master of Arts program in German at the University of Missouri-Columbia. Upon receiving my degree in 1968, the Viet Nam War was still raging, and I applied for and received a further deferment to pursue a doctorate in German at the University of Cincinnati, which prepared me for my career as a professor of German.

The limits of my language are the limits of my world.

—German philosopher, Ludwig Wittgenstein

To have another language is to possess a second soul.

—Charles the Great

A different language is a different vision of life.

—Federico Fellini, Italian filmmaker

NINE

THE STUDY OF GERMAN

I went off to college in search of myself or perhaps something which I could believe in, despite my dreams of excelling in school and achieving my goals having been derailed by a character named "Jim Crow," who had been created during the Reconstruction Period after the Civil War. The boogeyman Jim Crow stood between me and my dreams. I became hell bent on defeating him through achievement. I would make both Black and White proud of me through my accomplishments, in spite of all of obstacles set before me.

I was shaken from this internal lethargy when I heard the words, "Muska says that you are very good in German. Have you thought about majoring in German?" Kris Kogerma, a professor of German at

Berea College, greeted me with those words one day in Fall Semester 1963. I wondered why this White person with one of the sunniest dispositions I had ever known was showing a personal interest in me? His words certainly filled a personal deficit and an existential need that I had felt in the year or so I had been studying on campus. Given the closing of the public schools in Prince Edward County, the disruption of family and community life it caused, the question of whether I would get an education at all, and then living with a host-family and adhering to their rules to get an education, I didn't quite know where I was or who I was. I was struggling to find myself in a world of mostly White folks, with whom I shared no real-life experiences. I had come to Berea College looking for something that would presumably help me bridge the racial divide which had characterized my existence and that of other families in the community, something that would aid me in coming to terms with my potential hate of all White folk, because in my mind, *they (all of them) had done this to me*." They had blocked my route to an education, to a bright future where I could realize my full potential as a person. Through it all, in coming to terms with my value system, my father had taught my siblings and me that "one had to treat a person by the way they treated you, whether the person was Black or White." It was the "Golden Rule" right out of Pauline theology. From my perspective, this was a hard lesson to learn at the time.

I had been made aware of Berea College's commitment to racial justice since its founding in 1855 on the Berea Ridge by abolitionists six years before the beginning of the Civil War. Despite Berea College's moral commitment to the principle of interracial education, their experiment was interrupted when the State Legislature of Kentucky passed the Day Law in 1904 that forbade interracial education in the state. Whites could no longer study together with Blacks. This Law was not repealed until 1950.

So in addition to dealing with my own issues, I was part of the first group of Black students to study at Berea during the first dozen years after the Law's repeal. Most of the students at Berea at the time were White Southerners, some of whom certainly carried the weight and baggage of a segregated society because they had lived and breathed it, even if they did not subscribe to its tenants. The paradox is that they, too, had their existential challenges as far as the equality of the races was concerned. We all had to learn to incorporate Berea's motto into our lives and make it a part of us. We had to learn that "God had made of one blood all the peoples of the earth" (Acts 17:26).

Having excelled in math in high school, I had come to the institution intending to major in that discipline. Physics was not going well, in large part because the physics class I took in high school was inadequate. At least that was one of the factors. When the Board of Education of the segregated public schools of Mecklenburg County, Virginia, adopted a new updated physics book, they gave the updated texts to the White high school students. But rather than discard the outdated ones left in the office, they simply passed them on to the Black high school students.

So an invitation to choose a major in which I was excelling at least at the outset—*German*—held a promising prospect, despite the pushback from my parents and other family members. I had studied Latin for two years at a segregated high school in southern Virginia under a principal who believed in a solid traditional education. He insisted that Latin be offered despite the small size of the classes, which had ten to twelve students each. However, the experience with Latin made my encounter with German grammar a surmountable challenge, as I immediately understood and mastered the noun case system and the adjectival declension system, a sine qua non for any student serious about learning the German language. This has been a dogged challenge for many American students studying German, a fact I can attest to after teaching the language for nearly fifty years to first time learners who are native speakers of the English language.

My encounter with Professor Kogerma on Berea's campus in that fall of '63 was laced with irony. He was a White European male immigrant from Estonia who had experienced both the Nazis and the Russians and had fled his native country via Sweden for the United States. He was complimenting a Southern Black male, who had only known a segregated education, on his ability to begin mastering the German language. If he harbored any racial or ethnic prejudices, they were lost on me. His wife, whose acquaintance he first made in America, was a Lithuanian of German extraction who had also experienced the Nazis and the Russians in her home country.

Although they never shared any of these terrible experiences with me, I am certain that they were directly impacted by the occupations. This was the catalyst for their immigrating to the United States. When the Soviet Union annexed the three independent Baltic republics in 1940, they began their policy of sovietization and undertook mass deportations of the civilian population to forced settlements and forced labor camps inside the Soviet Union. When the Nazis defeated the Soviet Union in 1941, they were the second occupying power within a year's time. Immediately they began a campaign of repression, discrimination, mass deportations, and mass killings. When the Nazis were defeated and expelled from the Baltic republics by the Soviets in 1944, the Soviets resumed their policy of political repression, mass deportations, and mass executions. In the immediate postwar period, the Soviet Union annexed these republics and integrated them into the Soviet system, and they did not regain their independence until the fall of 1989 with the fall of the Berlin Wall and the breakup of the Soviet Union.

While the Kogermas no doubt experienced the German occupation, in their newfound home in America they became ambassadors of the German language and did a wonderful job of imparting it to their students. Mrs. Kogerma was my first teacher of German and was the "Muska" to whom Professor Kogerma referred with the endearing term. It never dawned on me that I was a member of an American minority group learning the language of the so-called "master race," the Nazi label for the German people, that I was learning the language of a people whose racially motivated and jingoistic leader preached hate against those who were different and almost wiped European Jewry from the face of Europe.

In hindsight of more than fifty years, I realize that not historical but existential motivation was the driving force in my life and uppermost in my mind. I was still trying to find out who I was and where I was going after the Prince Edward County experience. It had led to the disruption of my family's life and that of many others because of the need of us children to leave home earlier than expected in order to secure an education, which one expected to find in one's own community. These experiences challenged the development of my self-image in those years most crucial to its formation.

For me the "love affair" with the German language and most things German became my refuge. It also gave me the opportunity to show one-upmanship against fellow White students and to prove to myself that I could do "something special" that not everybody could do. And I excelled at it. It was a small triumph for me. The learning of German became the vehicle for me turning a liability into an asset, turning a loss into a gain.

By moving into another language and into a world where there was a new set of cues, where I was calling the shots or directing the program, so to speak, I was moving away from a negative cultural experience borne of American racism. Initially, I was becoming another person playing a role. In that space, I was able to find my way back to myself. Immersion in both the German culture and linguistic contexts gave me two positive vantage points from which I felt in control: I was the "outsider" looking in because I was not a German but a foreigner; at the same time, I was the "insider" pro tempore because I was conversant in the language and could theoretically and psychologically be somebody else, for a time at least. As ironic as it may seem, in the 1960s and 1970s I felt "more at home and more free" in Germany than in the United States because I could migrate to another world both linguistically and culturally where there was the sense of a new beginning, a "rebirth" existentially, as it were.

Lost on me at the time, is the irony in my experience as a Black American finding a comfort level in the language of a nation that less than thirty years earlier would not have welcomed me into their world. However, I was living in the moment and taking one day at a time; I was basking in adulation, which had been in short supply during my three-year ordeal away from the Prince Edward County public schools. At the time, it was about me, not about the Germans.

This plaque illuminates the history of the founding of Berea
College 1855 and the values for which it stood.

(Personal Collection)

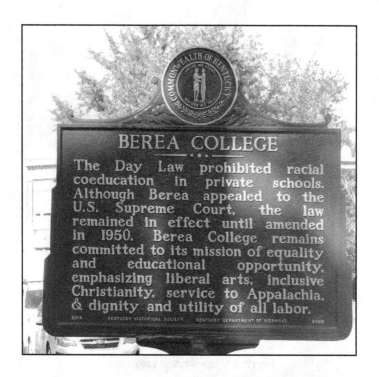

This plaque refers to the Day Law passed in 1904 prohibiting Blacks and Whites from attending school together. It was not repealed until 1950.

(Personal Collection)

I see my path, but I don't know where it leads.
Not knowing where I'm going is what
inspires me to travel it.

—Rosalinde Castro

There are no wrong turnings.
Only paths we had not known we were meant to travel.

—*Guy Gavriel Kay,* Tigana

TEN

CHARTING MY COURSE

While I felt good about my success in studying German at Berea, I was not quite sure what I would do with the major after graduation. The Kogermas had given me an opportunity to be a student assistant in the German program, so naturally they discussed with me the possibility of becoming a teacher of German. When I said to them that "Black folks are not interesting in learning German," they simply said, "teach White folks then." If I really wanted to go in that direction, I knew that I would need an advanced degree or two. Not sure how I would fare in a graduate program at one of the "high powered" departments that also offered a doctoral program, I decided to apply to the University of Missouri-Columbia which offered only a master's program. I thought that I would get more attention from the faculty there, and I did. In addition to enjoying small classes, I also got to try my hand at teaching German under another instructor's supervision. I became a graduate teaching assistant under the capable guidance of Mr. Joseph Blair, from whom I learned a great deal about teaching German. He was a gentle man and an exceptional pedagogue with lots of patience. The experience convinced me that I should apply to a doctoral program and consider the possibility of teaching German on the college level.

The doctoral program I ultimately chose was at the University of Cincinnati. From the outset, I felt it was the right fit for me for a number of reasons. The summer before entering the program, I made a visit to the department and indicated in an interview with the chair, Dr. Guy Stern, that I did not have the opportunity to study or work in Germany as an undergraduate student. He said that the department could perhaps help me with that, even as soon as the upcoming summer. He immediately called into his office the director of the University of Cincinnati Summer Program in Hamburg, Dr. Helga Slessarev, who smoothed the way for my participation that summer.

That summer of 1968, I lived with a family in the section of the city of Hamburg known as Blankenese and worked at a bookstore in Altona, one of the older sections in the city, where I had ample opportunity to improve my spoken German. My time in Germany bolstered my confidence in my spoken German and gave me an opportunity to experience life there for a couple of months.

The years spent as a graduate student, teaching assistant, and lecturer in Cincinnati were indeed wonderful. Not only was there a variety of interesting course offerings, there was also an energized and engaged community of people interested in "things German." The graduate student group consisted of Americans and naturalized Germans as well as exchange students from Germany, Austria, and Switzerland. The faculty was made up of a dynamic group of professors, supplemented each year by an exchange professor from Germany for one, two, or three quarters. (The university was still on the quarter system, mandated by the Ohio state university system.) I felt really "at home" at Cincinnati. One of the main factors contributing to this sense of belonging was the special friendship extended to me by Professor Edward P. Harris and his wife Marilyn, Southerners like myself, who understood and empathized with my anguish. They had studied at Millsaps College, a privately supported, liberal arts college in Jackson, Mississippi, known for its strong commitment to social justice. Professor and Mrs. Harris had come to Cincinnati imbued with this ethos, which made reaching out to me easy for them. They took me under their wing and offered me a home-away-from-home, so to speak. They often had me over for dinner and invited me to stop by when I wished or felt a need to do so. E.P., as he was affectionately known by his close friends, shared the same birthday with me as well as his taste for Classical music, which broadened my knowledge base on the subject and influenced my collection. As fate would have it, he ultimately became my dissertation advisor.

At Cincinnati I made many lasting friendships with White students in the program, and quickly improved my spoken German, as it was the preferred language used in and around the department. I also hung out with native speakers of German in my free time. The American graduate students were paired with graduate exchange students during their year abroad at Cincinnati to help smooth the transition to life as a graduate student in America. In the fall of 1971, I was paired with a German graduate student from Northwest Germany, Ludger Reiberg, who came for the year with his new bride, Christine Tonner-Reiberg, from Cologne. We quickly bonded, and they invited me to spend Christmas 1971 with their extended families in Germany. I met many members of both families and over the years my relationship with a number of them has developed into a lifelong friendship that is still strong today.

Professor Stern, departmental chair, saw my potential as a teacher and offered me a lectureship in German in 1970, which ultimately led to a position as an assistant professor in German at the University of Virginia in 1973, where I was placed in charge of the basic German language sequence and the supervision of the graduate teaching assistants. This was an extremely rewarding experience not only because of my supervisory role, but because at Virginia I had some of the best students I have ever had the privilege of teaching. Despite the positives, the Virginia experience was rife with challenges.

There was a paucity of Black faculty at the institution when I arrived. With the exception of two tenured faculty members in the English department, Arnold Rampersad and Houston Baker, who were keenly aware of their intellectual gifts and soon left Virginia for "greener pastures" and went on to become leading scholars in their field, the rest of us were junior faculty that did not have tenure and had very little political clout on campus. There was Romney Moseley in religious studies, Vivian Gordon in sociology, and myself in German. Later there were Ted Mason and Angela Davis in English, and George Starks in music. But of our group, only Vivian Gordon managed to receive tenure, and this was made possible because her chair, a well-known sociologist, had her co-author publications with him.

My association with the university ended when I did not receive continuing tenure there. With mixed emotions, I left the University of Virginia, and with those same feelings I accepted the teaching position at Wayne State University in Detroit. It was the only offer I received. The first couple of years at Wayne State were ones of great adjustment. However, after I found my stride, I had a wonderful experience during a long and distinguished career there. In addition to my teaching duties—which I thoroughly enjoyed, I also served as undergraduate advisor for more than twenty-five years, as master's advisor for a few years, and as acting chair of the department on several occasions.

While I served on numerous committees and panels at all levels of the university, a couple of them stand out for the important work that they performed. These committees had a direct impact on the undergraduate educational experience of the students at Wayne State. So I am particularly proud to have done this work. I served on the University's General Education

Oversight Committee for six years, during which time I served as chair of the Course Review Subcommittee. This subcommittee evaluated proposals submitted to meet the General Education course requirements for the basic undergraduate curriculum in all of the undergraduate colleges. The second committee was the Curriculum & Instruction Committee of the Academic Senate, on which I served for four years, two of them as chair. This committee worked very closely with the General Education Oversight Committee on courses that needed to go to the Academic Senate for discussion and approval.

For four years I served as an assistant provost and had in my portfolio the university's liaison to the gifted and talented program for Detroit Public Schools and international programs. The public school program offered enrichment courses on campus for the best and brightest of Detroit on Saturday mornings during the school year. These courses were taught mostly by tenure-track or tenured faculty so that high school students could get a feel for the college experience. Each spring there was a closing ceremony for the program and occasionally there was a snafu. From that experience I learned that one sometimes has to be a gopher despite one's title. On one occasion there were no chairs on stage despite the fact that they had been ordered. The provost and I rose to the occasion and took care of the job. A second aspect of the assignment which was totally unproblematic was registering students for dual enrollment courses at the university for which they got both high school and college credit simultaneously. I enjoyed this high school outreach job because it gave me an opportunity "to give back" to the Black community, since the student population in the Detroit Public Schools at the time was about 90% Black.

Having an interest in international programs and noting that Wayne State University had very few, I pushed for us to do more in terms of study abroad. This was not a topic of particular interest to the university president; however, he was interested in a reciprocity agreement with the University of Windsor (Canada), whereby students for either institution could take a select number of pre-approved courses offered by the other institution on a quid pro quo basis. At the time the Canadian students had to pay the out-of-state differential. The president was supportive of this initiative because of his interest in political science and Canadian studies. A couple of years after I moved to the Office of the Provost, the state of Michigan and the Japanese state of Shiga, which had signed a sister-state agreement in 1968, established the Japan Center for Michigan Universities in Shiga Prefecture, whose mission was to offer ESL instruction to Japanese students and a year's study abroad in Japan to students from all 15 Michigan state universities who were interested in learning or furthering their Japanese studies. Since Japanese was not offered at Wayne State at that time, I was asked to be Wayne State's representative to the consortium. In this role I was able to travel to Japan for the opening and dedication of the center in 1989. It was a wonderful and most rewarding experience, and I became a "student of Japanese culture" during the visit.

A couple of things struck me as an American. Japan is a very conformist society. For example, when crossing the street, all obey the signs "almost religiously." No one would dare jaywalk. I observed this in a group of school children waiting quietly at a street crossing. When two of my colleagues and I traveled by train from Shiga to Kyoto, several small children on the train pointed fingers at us and then hid their faces in a "hide and seek" manner to the chagrin of their mothers, who were embarrassed and tried subtly to dissuade them from such behavior. I was also struck by the fact that cremation in Japan is a universal norm as in all Asian cultures, which means that the grave markers are very close to one another. With my sometimes silly sense of humor, I remarked that the Japanese "bury their dead standing up," which brought loads of laughter from the other Michigan university representatives and state dignitaries on a bus tour in the Shiga area.

Outside the institution, I served for a number of years as a Reader for the College Board's Advanced Placement Test in German. Before that experience I would have disputed anyone that essays can be graded objectively. As a Reader I learned that criteria had been developed that one could indeed use to evaluate the essays critically, objectively and fairly. In fact, we were tested against ourselves to ensure reliability of scores. And any Reader who did not do well on the test would not be invited back to a subsequent reading. The work of reading and evaluating the essays was challenging, and since the German group was small— never more than twelve—it was important that a sense of teamwork always prevailed. All of us were careful to recommend colleagues whom we thought and hoped had even temperaments and got along well with others, at which we on occasion failed. During my tenure as a Reader, the group met at Trenton State and Clemson. Although the pay for the work was nominal, we looked forward to the work and the camaraderie. We lived in the dormitories and ate in the dining hall, so it felt a bit like we were in summer camp. All in all, it was a most enjoyable experience which we looked forward to each summer. For two years I served on the Test Development Committee for AP German, which gave me quite a bit of insight into the process of test development and all of the elements and considerations that go into its design. I learned that all test items are put through rigorous review and meet the highest standards for quality and fairness. Once the test is completed, it has to be pre-tested and the feedback evaluated, before the new version of the exam can be released. For this work we met at Educational Testing Service headquarters in Princeton, N.J.

In addition to my other activities and responsibilities during my time at Wayne State University, I managed to publish two books: *The Image of America in Postwar German Literature: Reflections and Perceptions* (1982), and *Migrants' Literature in Postwar Germany: Trying to Find a Place to Fit In* (2006). Both publications deal with issues of identity, which has been an abiding research focus of mine. This interest was no doubt motivated by my quest for an authentic self, and my existential journey after the Prince Edward County experience. In 1974 and 1982 respectively, I received summer Fulbright awards to the Federal Republic of Germany.

One of the most rewarding experiences of my thirty-four-year career at the university was the year spent at

University of Freiburg in the Black Forest region, where I served as resident director of the WSU Junior Year in Freiburg Program for the academic year 1995-96. It was a consortium program with the University of Michigan at Ann Arbor, the University of Wisconsin at Madison, and Michigan State University. During this wonderful and rewarding year in Freiburg the students had the normal problems usually associated with a study abroad program, but nothing out of the ordinary. The major challenge for me was the nervous breakdown suffered by the administrative assistant at the beginning of the winter semester. I found myself managing all of the chores in the office, including the bookkeeping. Having worked as a student office manager at Audio Visual Service at Berea, and having taken an accounting course one summer after moving to Detroit, I was able to handle with ease the financial details of the program and prepare the accounting documents to send to WSU for reconciliation.

Directing this program gave me an opportunity for validation by professionals not directly associated with Wayne State University, which I found very rewarding. As a program director, I was invited to all of the important events and ceremonies related to academics at the university, among them, the official opening of the academic year 1995-96 with the installation of a new rector, which is more or less equivalent to the president of an American university. Outside the university community, I also received invitations to events sponsored by municipal and civic groups. For example, I was among the invited guests of the mayor's office to the official opening and dedication of the *Konzerthaus* Freiburg.

In reflecting back on my teaching, service, and research career of nearly fifty years—forty-four as a professor and three as a graduate teaching assistant, I can say that my life in academia was a most satisfying and rewarding one. It afforded me wonderful life experiences that I never could have imagined when the lights were turned out on public education for Blacks in Prince Edward County, or when I was an insecure and struggling student at Berea College in the early '60s.

The road to becoming one of a handful of university-level Black professors of German in the '70s was not an easy one. The bumps in the road along the way never let me forget the burdens of racism and how it affects everyone, no matter which side you're on. My first job after leaving graduate school at the University of Cincinnati was at the University of Virginia, which I began in 1973. I felt that I was returning to

Virginia triumphant after having been denied a high school education in my native state, particularly since I was coming as a professor of German to the flagship university that would not have accepted me as an undergraduate in 1962—the year I received my high school diploma. The first Black undergraduates were accepted in the UVA College of Arts and Sciences in 1963. Despite my feeling of victory, I still had mixed emotions and a chip on my shoulder. And of course, there was the underlying fear that I would not be "made welcome in the house," so to speak.

It does not surprise me in retrospect that an encounter with a young White male student from the South would upset my equilibrium and cause the experience of past racism to raise its ugly head. One day at the end of my beginning German class, one of my best students, a young blond fellow from Alabama came up to me and asked me if I was a native German. Although I am fair skinned, I look nothing like a German. Given my physical appearance and the fact that I was back in the Commonwealth of Virginia, I took umbrage to the inquiry and asked him, "Do I look like a German?" I realized then that the chip I had on my shoulder because of the experience of racism in Virginia was still there, that I was still shaping "my new self" with a piece of the puzzle that had been missing—missing since the time of the public schools closing in Prince Edward County and most likely repressed during the time I spent outside the state. I had come full circle, looking at myself in the mirror of the past and could not see beyond that point in time. It turned out that this student was from a well-to-do Southern family of means and privilege, but he harbored not an iota of racism. He had been born and raised in Alabama during the Civil Rights Movement of the '60s and had been sensitized to the problems and challenges of race relations in the South. Rather than taking a defensive posture, the young man remarked that my German sounded like that of native Germans, whom he had heard speaking when his family had gone on a European trip. He suggested that it did not sound anything like that of the stereotyped German characters found in "Hogan's Heroes," the second-rate television series based loosely on Nazi history. My experience with the student from Alabama was one that got me moving again on the road to finding my own unique existential identity from which the negative experience of racism had derailed me.

Among my duties at Virginia was the supervision of the graduate teaching assistants in German. Ironically, not one eyebrow was raised by students, graduate or undergraduate, but by some members of the White faculty who had difficulty accepting the fact that I had a doctorate in German. If it were in French or Spanish that would be fine, for after all, France and Spain had a long experience with colonialism, and the citizens of their former colonies spoke the language of the colonialists. Germany, on the other hand, had limited experience with colonialism in East and Southwest Africa, only beginning in the 1890s and coming to an end shortly after World War I. This incredulity on the part of some White institutional faculty was also put to the test in "polite society" outside the university's grounds when some of the German faculty, including me, were invited to a reception by a low-level German countess who asked me, "Do you speak German?"

I could not know if my German hostess's presupposition that a Black professor of German at the University of Virginia might not speak German was based on her ignorance of American institutions of higher learning, whether she had grown up in Hitler's Nazi Germany and fully subscribed to his Aryan doctrine that non-Aryans were inferior people and could not possibly master the German language, or whether she was just naïve, ignorant, or had had her perception influenced by the prevailing racial atmosphere in Charlottesville, where a definite separation between "town and gown" existed. Naturally I was taken aback by the remark, felt insulted, and was speechless in the moment. A German-Jewish colleague of mine "blessed her soul" to such an extent that I suspect that she was left to ponder the blessing long after the event was over.

One summer as a participant in a faculty Summer Fulbright Seminar in Germany, one of the docents for the program said to me, "Of all the non-native speakers in the program, your German is the best!" I took umbrage taking it as condescension. My response was, "Why do you say that? Are you surprised?" I am not sure that she detected the touch of sarcasm in my response. Her response was simply, "It is not a compliment but a fact." At that, I began to realize that Germans in general do not hand out gratuitous compliments like we Americans do. This is clearly a cultural difference between Germans and Americans.

One summer when I gave a talk at an international conference in Berlin, the German participants were impressed with my German skills and did not want to believe that an American—they didn't say Black American—who had not grown up in Germany could have mastered the German language so well that he had practically no foreign accent. I felt agitated, and my lesser self got the best of me. I told them, "My grandmother was German." I don't know what they thought after that remark because there was no more discussion of the issue. From that point forward and on repeated occasions, I got compliments about how well I had mastered the German language and was told that I had near native fluency.

Over the years, I have come to realize that my success has been based on several factors: the mastery of all of the major aspects of the German language system, a certain affinity for learning foreign languages, particularly German because of what I see as its "mathematical" properties, and, finally, the passion and enthusiasm with which I have pursed something in which I can excel. If those factors had not been operative, it is dubious whether I would have been as successful. After all, I was nineteen years of age when I began studying German.

I have had the good fortune of having lasting friendships with Germans in the Federal Republic for nearly fifty years. This has contributed richly to me personally and professionally because it has given me the opportunity to perfect my German speaking skills and experience German cultural institutions firsthand. When I think of these friendships, members of the Reiberg family extended come to mind. Over the years they have offered love, support, and friendship. They have always received me with open arms and have never treated me as an outsider on the numerous trips I have made to the Federal Republic. They have confirmed for me on countless occasions that my German skills are excellent; that those who complimented me were neither condescending nor passing out empty and gratuitous accolades.

Dr. Alfred L. Cobbs majored in German at Berea: "I was trying to find my voice," he says. Now a German professor at Wayne State University in Detroit, he won the President's award for Excellence in Teaching in 1984, and has won two Fulbright scholarships.

15

Photo taken of me at Wayne State University.

(M.J. Murawka)

Photo taken of me in 2006 in my office at Wayne State University.

(M.J. Murawka)

*A well-prepared and engaging teacher is a catalyst ...
a spark that creates the desire to learn in our students.*

—Robert John Meeham

*When the untapped potential of a student meets
the liberating art of a teacher, a miracle unfolds.*

—Mary Hatwood Futrell

ELEVEN

THE LOVE OF TEACHING AND ITS REWARDS

My love of the German language and things German grew into a passion over the years. And in teaching German studies full-time for nearly half a century that passion never dissipated; indeed, it was a "labor of love." The passion and enthusiasm exuded, however, is meaningless if it does not energize and motivate those whom one is trying to reach. Over the years, I was never quite sure whether I was achieving my goals. My true blessing is that students have felt it and expressed it over the years. At the time of my retirement a number of them put these comments in writing for my retirement booklet, from which I cite some excerpts:

"Professor Cobbs was an inspiration to all because of his passion to teach the German language."

"Your passion in what you do is inspiring and a benchmark on how I rate my other professors."

"I learned so much during our German class, and though it was challenging, it was the best class I have ever had."

"He was a great mentor not only because he had great teaching ability and knowledge of the subject, but because he had great enthusiasm about the subject matter."

A year after I retired, I received, out of the blue, an email from a former student who had encountered me as a professor in the mid-1980s. It had been more than twenty-five years after he had been a German student of mine. I was struck by the unsolicited praise that he heaped upon me and my teaching with the hindsight of a quarter century. While I had never been one to put too much stock in the students' comments on the evaluation forms at the end of the semester, I would take the statement quoted below "to the bank with me," for it was unsolicited after all of these years. The student wrote,

Over the years since my time with you as a mentor, I have often thought about your admonition that

people should not 'rest on their laurels.'

Success for me has been driven by the desire to do something more than I did yesterday, to excel in new ways and conquer fresh challenges.

I wish I could adequately explain how much your teaching and mentoring opened my eyes to what was possible in life. You gave me gifts so far beyond what I expected to find in that first German 101 class!

He continued with the following: *"Today, I am still working as a classical tenor; I also have a private voice studio where I train singers from all over the country ... I think of you often as I teach, wondering if I can inspire my students the way you inspired me so many years ago."*

After having received such positive and inspiring feedback from several of my former students, I went back to look at some of the comments students wrote on my behalf when I was nominated for and received the President's Award for Excellence in Teaching from Wayne State University in 1984. Students who supported my nomination wrote:

"He challenges his students to achieve the highest degree of excellence."

"Dr. Cobbs is a superb instructor. His enthusiasm is infectious."

"He cares about his students, and even though he

is very demanding, he makes you want to learn. He does not crush the spirit."

I lost myself in something I was extremely passionate about, overcame some adversity along the way, found refuge, and in the end, found myself, too. It was a life-changing experience. That is exactly what I needed when the German professor at Berea approached me and talked of Muska's positive evaluation of my learning the German language. At the time, they both believed in me and saw a potential that I could not and did not see in myself. Such mentors and role models inspire us and lift us to heights that we cannot imagine initially. In writing for my retirement from my position as a professor of German at Wayne State University, my friend and colleague, professor Hans-Peter Söder, resident director of the our Junior Year in Munich Program, wrote, I think, in a very elegant way, about how studying German transformed my life—describing how it set my spirit free and helped me to find my way back to myself. He writes:

... *the story of how Alfred Cobbs overcame the adversity and racism of 1960s America to teach America's students about the ideals of German classicism, is real. The accounting of the setting free of one man's spirit is worth telling and re-telling, if only to demonstrate that literature has real and lasting effects on our lives. Alfred Cobbs has made a difference in the lives of generations of Americans.*

Given my dedication to, and love for, what I was blessed to do for a career, retiring has been a hard parting of ways. However at the end of a happy and fulfilling career and a life filled with joy and many rewards, there are moments of wistfulness for those professors of German at Berea, the Kogermas, who helped me find my way but had their lives cut short, suffering a fate more terrible than what might have befallen them at the hands of the Nazis and the Russians. In an ugly stroke of irony, they came to their demise at the hands of their own blood. One of their 24-year-old twin sons murdered them in 1975 when they were in their early fifties and the prime of life. The terrible incident took place on Mrs. Kogerma's fifty-second birthday.

Now and then I still have sobering thoughts when I think about the fact that the Kogermas invested their time, their energy and their love in someone's son who was lost and needed help finding his way and his equilibrium, yet they could neither help nor save their own wayward son from himself and a world of darkness and mental distress that would lead him to commit such a dastardly act. I knew him as a loving and bright child and have never been able to fully come to terms with it. The trigger that set off the killing spree was the Kogermas' attempt to get their son to return to psychiatric care in Lexington, Kentucky, having failed to convince him to recommit himself voluntarily. In the *Berea Citizen* article, writer Dorothy Shearard, refers to the neighbors' perception of the Kogermas' anguish about their son's mental state: "Neighbors say that young [*name omitted*] was showing increasing signs of possible mental disturbance, and that the family was attempting to get him to return to hospital care on his own volition. The parents were particularly anxious, neighbors said, not to force the young man into treatment" (*Berea Citizen*, June 11, 1975).

There is a further irony in this dark event that had a profound effect on me. I had signed a contract with Berea College to begin teaching there in 1973, and it is a possibility that I might have been visiting my former professors and having tea with them on the day they were murdered. After all, it was Mrs. Kogerma who introduced me to the wonderful teas from India, *Assam and Darjeeling*, and from China, *Kemun and Oolong*. But fate was kinder to me. I had broken the contract with Berea College when the opportunity arose to teach at the University of Virginia—something I had to do for the sake of the family, the history of the University, and race relations in the Commonwealth of Virginia. My blessing is that my father lived to see me begin my teaching career at the state's flagship university before he slipped away from us less than six months after my return to Virginia. Although he never told me how proud he was of me and my accomplishments, he certainly told several White farmers, for whom we had done day labor. They told me about it after my father's death. In fact, one of the farmers, whose son was studying at the university's School of Business at the time, asked his son to look me up in my office on campus, to make my acquaintance, and bring me greetings from his father. Upon our meeting, he accorded me the proper respect due to a professor by a student. Despite the racism that permeated and still permeates American society, I could detect their pride in my accomplishments, even if they did not state it outright. Maybe this is what Daddy meant when he used to say, "One day the bottom rail will come to the top."

I remember once hearing one of my role models, Dr. W. Gordon Ross, a professor of philosophy and religion at Berea, deliver a sermon at Sunday Night Chapel about a man who found his calling in life as a missionary in Southeast Asia. I have long forgotten the details of the sermon, but it was clear from the message that in the eyes of the world he was a "second place winner" because his work did not make a big splash or bring him titles or accolades. His "service" to others, however, made him a "first place winner" as far as humanity and the ultimate scheme of things are concerned. I carried the message of this sermon with me after I left Berea and it remained with me throughout my long career. While I did not achieve the highest rank or accolades at my academic institution, I now know in retrospect that the "service" I gave to students and for the institution as a whole via committee work—a value inculcated at Berea College—in my role as a professor of German was the most important gift that professors can bestow upon their students. What I did as a "second place winner" in the eyes of my peers and colleagues made me a "first place winner" in the eyes of those whom I was privileged to serve for nearly fifty years—the students.

My striving was to give my best and to reach every student regardless of what they brought to the table. In some cases that was a challenge, since not all students who took German with me were happy campers—especially those taking it as a requirement and wanted to simply get it behind them as soon as possible.

My success was tempered by a sobering experience I had trying to teach a student German at the beginning of my career. In Fall Semester 1969, I had been appointed as a lecturer in German at the University of Cincinnati and faced my first lesson in humility and failure—one of the greatest lessons a teacher can learn. I would come to realize this decades later in a conversation about assessments and outcomes. As a neophyte lecturer in German, I was challenged to help a Black student who was struggling with learning German. Eager to help him, I proceeded with all of my grammar explanations in English and its application to German. But the student still didn't understand! I met with him several times more and the "pump did not produce water." To this day, I remember pouring out my heart to a young fellow German instructor about my failure. But he had no answer for me, although he was both empathetic and sympathetic to my dilemma and frustration. I don't know whether it was my inability to reach the student or his inability to learn German, or whether there were other forces at work. I just know that this experience forced me to look deeply inward, to do some introspection about my teaching. From that day forward, after each class I conducted a post mortem to reflect on what succeeded and what failed, what I might have done better or more efficiently, and if I had reached those who wanted to be reached.

*Photo taken on May 9, 2014, at the luncheon celebrating
my retirement from Wayne State University.*

(Laura Kline)

We don't develop courage by being happy every day.
We develop it by surviving difficult times
and challenging adversity.

—*Barbara De Angelis*

The light at the end of the tunnel is not an end
but a beginning of something new.

—*Prashant Ingole*

TWELVE

DARK DAYS

During my elementary school days in Prince Edward County we sometimes had substitute teachers, whose job was basically to keep order since they had not prepared for the class with the lesson plans of the classroom teacher. I remember one particular substitute who was wheelchair bound, blind, and wore dark glasses, Rev. Arthur Jordon. In his conversations with the class, I remember him saying that in life there would be "some dark days." As a boy of ten or eleven years of age, I had no idea how true I would find his words as I matured. This lesson dovetailed well with something my father used to say about the vicissitudes of life, "keep on living."

In 1962, after receiving my diploma from a still

segregated high school located a hundred miles from the one where I should have graduated, I had a need to leave the Commonwealth of Virginia. Moton High School, from which I should have graduated, stood padlocked with signs in front reading "No Trespassing." I felt defeated and only by leaving the state could I deal with the hate that might have festered in me had I remained there. I had to square those feelings with a couple of lessons I had learned from home: never hate anyone, and only judge people, both Black and White, by how they treat us. So I left Virginia to pursue undergraduate studies at Berea College in Kentucky. Following the Berea experience, I attended the University of Missouri and then the University of Cincinnati for graduate study.

After having completed my graduate studies, I returned to the Commonwealth of Virginia as a professor of German studies at the University of Virginia in Charlottesville. I felt triumphant. I thought I had it made. I was accepted graciously by the German-area faculty there, and I seemed to have no problem being accepted by the students. But I was not equipped for that world where the "old boy network" had awarded tenure to faculty less qualified than I, with slim or non-existent publishing records. Be that as it may, as women and minorities joined the ranks of the faculty, the requirements for tenure were ratcheted up, not only at UVA but across many institutions around the country, and during my six years at Virginia, only one of fewer than a dozen Black faculty members received tenure. Vivian Gordon, a Black woman in sociology, had the strong support of her chair and had co-authored publications with him. Admittedly, I only had a slim publication record at the time. My labor-intensive work focused on establishing a program in basic German language and training the new incoming teaching assistants. I took my work seriously and threw myself intensely into it. My colleagues assured me that they were sympathetic to my plight and would fight for me when I came up for tenure. There were professors at both Berkeley and Stanford who had jobs similar to mine and were given tenure at the rank of "senior lecturer" because they had limited publication records. However, when the moment of truth arrived, all of my tenured German colleagues "jumped ship." In retrospect, I realize I was naïve about the rigid and conservative nature of the tenure system.

I felt totally defeated by the turn of events and did not know which way forward. Shortly thereafter I spent the weekend with family in the countryside where I grew up, and my sister Patsy, upon hearing my story, simply said to me, "Oh, you will get another job." Her words turned out to be true. I did get another job as a professor of German, but it was not an easy road. To add insult to injury, that sixth year at Virginia, the chair of the department, without my permission and without speaking to me directly, asked one of the tenured colleagues to take over my duties when I left, and promised him that he could use the teaching materials I had developed. Because that colleague and I were not on the best of terms, he also did not discuss the issue with me. He, too, acted in a disrespectful and cowardly way and went to my teaching assistants behind my back and asked them for the material. Having developed a sense of loyalty to me over the course of our working relationship, the teaching assistants came to me and asked what they should do. I told them that under no circumstances should they give the colleague the materials. If he wanted to use them, he should come to me and ask my permission.

It all led to a confrontation between the chair and me, in which I asserted my dignity and defended my integrity, two qualities I will never allow anyone to take from me—on that there is no compromise. Power and wealth I may never have, but dignity and integrity I will carry with me to the grave. The chair tried to use the power of the office to coerce me into giving in to his request and expectations by trying to censor me in front of my colleagues at a German-area faculty meeting. Fortunately, I knew of this plan just before the meeting because one of the secretaries in the department, who had typed the letter, presented it to me just before I walked into the meeting. In the letter the chair expressed his disappointment in what he viewed as my uncooperative spirit.

At the meeting, he presented the case as a hypothetical one involving a conflict between two colleagues and expressed his view on the matter. Things backfired on him, however, as other colleagues expressed different perspectives. Enraged, the chair asked me to come to his office after the meeting and began to castigate and threaten me with words to the effect that he could ruin my career. My dander was now up, my dignity was at stake, and my integrity was challenged. After he had said his piece, I, now in a state of rage, let him know in no uncertain terms that he could not ruin my career because my life did not depend on my having a career as a professor of German. I informed him that I would dig ditches if I had to rather than surrender my dignity for a job. In that moment, he was incredulous and opined that I had misunderstood his intent. I was no fool; I had prevailed. In that moment, I knew who I was, from where I had come, and where I was headed.

In the fall of 1978, I applied for or wrote letters

of inquiry to nearly 150 institutions about a possible opening in German, in preparation of my fall 1979 departure from UVA. The only invitation for a campus visit came from Wayne State University in Detroit; they asked me to come in February, not the best time of the year to visit a city in the Lower Midwest. When I arrived in Detroit, the luggage did not arrive with me, no doubt because of a delay in the transfer in Washington, DC, from Piedmont Airlines to Northwest Orient Airlines during inclement winter weather. After the chair, Professor Marvin Schindler, picked me up, we went to dinner at a restaurant in the Book Cadillac Hotel in downtown Detroit. We sat in a booth, and upon our leaving, I tore my suit pants just below the crotch. The next day I would have to meet the departmental faculty and give a teaching demonstration with torn pants. How to accomplish this while teaching proved to be an interesting challenge. I backed up rather than turned around; and whenever I wrote on the board (yes, professors did that in the age before computers), I turned myself so that the torn side was toward the board and the undamaged side was toward the students, who must have thought that I was a bit weird. But with a group of professors sitting in the back row observing my teaching, it was really not a normal class anyway. The suitcase arrived the next day, and I was able to change clothes to make my appearance before the dean of the college.

I got the job at Wayne State University in Detroit— the only offer I received out of the nearly 150 applications I submitted to institutions of higher education. The first year was traumatic. Just ten years out from the riots of 1968, the city was a long way from recovering. Needing somewhere to live, I decided to look for a house in the city. I wanted to buy into a co-op downtown in a section of houses designed by the famous German-Jewish architect, Mies van der Rohe, of *Bauhaus* fame, who immigrated to the United States during the Nazi period. However, one needed $20,000.00 to purchase equity in the property. I did not have the funds, and no one in the family was in a position at the time to lend me what I needed to make up the shortfall. So I settled for a house in a Detroit neighborhood that had not suffered much White flight after the riots, was fairly stable, and integrated. To purchase the property, I added a couple thousand dollars to the $14,000.00 profit I had made on the small house I held for three years in Charlottesville. My mistake was putting down such a large sum to purchase the house, which left me a bit cash strapped. When interest rates skyrocketed to seventeen percent under the Carter Administration, I was in a real cash crisis.

I soon discovered that this house, similar to my first house in Charlottesville, needed a new roof and a furnace. The roof was leaking over the entrance due to flashings that needed replacing, and the monstrous old furnace, converted from coal to gas, was inefficient. The heating bills were much larger than they would have been with a more efficient furnace. On top of unforeseen housing expenses, the transmission seal on my car needed replacing. I kept spotting drops of oil on the driveway. I made the mistake of taking it to an Aamco Transmission facility where I "was taken" right away and knew it. But once I was in the hands of a crook, I felt trapped. I was told I needed a new transmission which cost me well over five hundred dollars, which I didn't have. I was being careful about adding to my Visa credit card balance, since it was a bit overloaded at that time because of the move. To make matters worse, some faculty and staff at Wayne State University were being given "pink slips" and some contracts for non-tenured faculty were being terminated. Needless to say, I was stressed out. At the time Wayne State was having budgetary issues. I had already been told I would not be receiving raises in my second and probably the third year.

With the help of my brother, Freddie, and his wife, Pattie, I moved into my new house right around Labor

Day. When they left me, I was on my own in a city where I had no family or friends, and I did not yet know any neighbors. The house was without a refrigerator and stove. Since the neighbors were not particularly welcoming, and I needed ice, I decided to go to Highland Appliance to buy a refrigerator and a stove, hoping they would be delivered in a couple of days. Although I had a credit card, the salesman would not accept it for the purchase because I did not have a Michigan driver's license; the one from Virginia was unacceptable. I had to go the next day to a bank and withdraw enough cash to pay for the appliances before they were delivered. The new gas stove, a reputable *Caloric*, began to act up before I ever used it. On the day of its arrival, while sitting at the kitchen table, I heard a gushing sound as if gas was being turned on. Indeed, the oven would simply come on at random with no prompting. I immediately called the store to report it and was told that no one could come out until after Labor Day. I used every curse word in my vocabulary and said that if the house blew up because of the problem my family would sue the company for all it was worth! My threat somehow worked, and a repairman was sent out the same day to take care of the problem.

Once classes started at Wayne State University, I realized I was working with a much different group of students. They were much more tentative and fragile than the students I had worked with and challenged at the University of Virginia. I came to realize that the issues the students at Wayne State had to balance made their lives as students very difficult. Most were the first generation in their families to go to college, and most had to work to pay for schooling. They often lived at home and had to support family members or other needs within the family. Often they had to make a choice between the needs of one family member or another and their schooling. They found me to be too critical and surly for their taste. I felt devastated by this honest critique because the students at UVA found me to be an excellent, if difficult teacher. To add fuel to the fire and to make the picture even darker, Mama had been diagnosed with colorectal cancer and was dying of it. She also was carrying my burden because I told her how unhappy I was in Detroit. When she died in 1982, three years after my move from Charlottesville to Detroit, I was devastated. When my German colleague and friend, Uwe Faulhaber, saw how depressed I was, he said that maybe we should trade places. I did not at first understand what I felt was such a strange statement. A year later after I had received tenure, he invited me to lunch. I almost lost my appetite when he explained his strange and cryptic statement of a year earlier. He informed me that he had leukemia, and his chances of survival were 50/50, even if he had the bone marrow transplant at the Mayo Clinic, as a doctor friend from his Oberlin days who worked at the Clinic advised him he needed. He lived only a couple years more before he succumbed to the illness.

During the years that he was being treated, he remained so upbeat. He became my spiritual inspiration and always lifted me whenever I was in his presence. He was a man of high intellect, humility, good cheer, and a heart of gold. He could tell when I was unhappy by just looking at me. He would tell me that I needed "people to love me" and indicated that his kids loved me. He would invite me to dinner with him and the kids. He always prepared the dinner himself because his wife, Cindy, attended evening law school classes. Noting my unhappiness, it was Uwe who convinced me to seek counseling to help me deal with my depression and unhappiness. He informed me that he was seeing a psychiatrist to deal with his impending death. When he was having blood transfusions at the Detroit Medical Center, I would pick him up at home during the noon hour and drive him to the hospital. Every time I picked him up, I asked him how he was doing. He always redirected the conversation by saying "don't ask about me, tell me how you are doing?" And he would on occasion ask me to stop somewhere so that he could buy chocolates for the nurses, technicians, and other professionals who treated him. Despite his own situation, he never lost his humanity; his focus was always directed away from himself and toward others.

Uwe told me that whatever I could do to find happiness and inner peace, I should do so. I took his advice, but I didn't want anyone in my circle of colleagues at the university or members and friends from my church to know that I was undergoing psychological counseling. I made the decision to drive the forty-three miles each way twice per week to attend group sessions at the Life Stress Center in Ann Arbor. Dr. Ruediger, a former priest, and his colleague Diane, a psychological social worker, were instrumental in helping me deal with my stress and find my way back to myself. What I learned from those sessions was that I was too self-critical and too much of a perfectionist for my own good. Further, I learned that I needed to exorcise deep-seated trauma. Dr. Ruediger told me that I was angry at somebody and suggested that it might be my father. I asked him how could I be angry with a person who was dead. His response was that "the feeling is still real." That of course made me furious, and I had the urge to slap him, which he invited me to do. Of course, I would not dare do that, but the group session helped me to deal with the anguish in my belly and bring it to the light of day. Once I did that, the boogeyman was gone.

At one of the sessions, Dr Ruediger asked me what the second commandment was, and I stumbled to find the obvious answer: "Thou shall love thy neighbor as thyself." It was as if the scales fell from my eyes in an instant. "One cannot love others if one does not love oneself unconditionally, with all of one's failings and imperfections." My "as thyself" moment occurred sometime in the 1980s and from that day forward my darkness turned to light, despite the challenges that I faced and those sure to come. But through this new perspective, I learned that I am not a victim and that adversity and challenges are normative and happen to all of us to a greater or lesser degree. After that life-changing moment, my teaching improved, and I got closer to my students. They came to see that in spite of my "tough love," I had their best interest at heart. And in 1984, I won the President's Award for Excellence in Teaching at Wayne State University, which could not have happened without positive feedback from my students.

*Moton High School padlocked, the driveway cordoned off,
and a sign posted warning students and others to keep their
distance from the school property.*

(Edward Peoples Collection, Virginia Commonwealth University)

In the end, reconciliation is a spiritual process,
which requires more than a legal framework.
It has to happen in the hearts and minds of people.

—*Nelson Mandela*

THIRTEEN

RECONCILIATION
AND PEACE

I f the summer of 1959 was a low point in race relations, I was hopeful July 21, 2008, would be a turning point. As I stood on the lawn of Virginia's State Capitol in Richmond, once the capital of the Confederate States of America, and in the mind of many White Southerners a hallowed ground for White folks only, it became clear to me that this was, indeed, a historic moment in race relations in the Commonwealth of Virginia. For the first time in its history, the Virginia State Legislature agreed to have constructed on the Capitol grounds a monument to the contributions of Black Virginians who had played key roles in the Civil Rights Movement.

Its unveiling and dedication that day attracted a large crowd—an audience of nearly four thousand people.

The ceremony took place on a very warm sunny July afternoon in Richmond under a canopy of trees in sight of the Virginia State Capitol building, whose grounds had been manicured perfectly for the occasion. There was not a cloud in the sky. The crowd was upbeat and there was a sense of pride, excitement, and anticipation as they took in the events of the day. When it was all over, the crowd dispersed, happy and pleased to have witnessed this act of reconciliation with regards to race relations in the Commonwealth of Virginia.

On the front panel of the monument is the figure of Barbara Johns, the 16-year-old girl from Prince Edward County who led the school boycott in 1951; she is flanked by others who joined her in the strike. On one of the side panels is the figure of the Rev. Lester Francis Griffin, Jr., the lone voice among clergy in the community, either Black or White, who supported the student strike. On the other side panel are the figures of the civil rights attorneys Oliver W. Hill and Spottswood W. Robinson III, who spearheaded the case as it went to the Supreme Court as one of the litigants in the *Brown v. Board of Education* portfolio in 1951. And the back panel, alluding to the future, is the depiction of an integrated school population.

I watched as several thousand others took it all in, against the backdrop of Prince Edward County deciding to abolish public education in the county in 1959 rather than desegregate, an action sanctioned by the Virginia State Legislature in 1954. Their behavior had been a clear act of defiance of the federal mandate and a demonstration of Virginia's "massive resistance" effort to ignore or nullify anything that did not conform to its view of Civil Rights in the Commonwealth.

Because of this action, the lives of many fellow students had been forever disrupted or scarred. Their God-given potential had been "nipped in the bud," like a plant that had been pruned too soon and left to wither and die. Some young people did not get the "second chance" or a "reprieve" like my two brothers and I did.

What happened later that day in Farmville, the seat of Prince Edward County government, would tax my emotions almost to the breaking point, for it was almost impossible for me to grasp that what was happening was real and not a dream. There was a program with a banquet and a public lighting ceremony to commemorate the Prince Edward County tragedy. The ceremony, with the title "Illumination Ceremony of the Light of Reconciliation," took place on the lawn in front of the county court house. At that time the Board of Supervisors, now made up of both Black and White members, apologized publicly for their 1959 predecessors. They admitted the mistake and expressed genuine regret to the Black community for the irreparable damage done to it by their action. The event also paid homage to strike leader Barbara Rose Johns as well as to the other children in the county who played a pivotal and historic role in ending public school segregation in the United States. As a gesture of the seriousness of their commitment, a marker was placed on the courthouse lawn on which the apology is visible for all to see.

The ceremony took place in the late afternoon after the banquet at Longwood University. The heat of the earlier part of the day had increased and it was now sweltering, despite the fact that the event was held outside and the evening was moving into sunset. The event was staged later in the afternoon so that there would be sufficient darkness to allow illumination of the cupola. Many in the crowd were sweating profusely, and the mood of the crowd was somber and pensive. Due to the sweat that drenched my body, the dye in my necktie faded into the fabric of the shirt I was wearing and ruined it. One of the ironies of this reconciliation ceremony is the fact that Barbara Johns's sister Joan shared the stage with the daughter of J. Barry Wall, a diehard segregationist and editor of the *Farmville*

Herald at the time of the school strike. However, there was no animus between the relatives of two people who in the '50s and '60s would not have been willing to share the stage with one another under any circumstances.

In addition to the ceremony and the unveiling, they also illuminated the eternal light of reconciliation, which they had placed in the cupola of the courthouse. This was the first time that this kind of gesture was ever made in the county for any occasion. So the reaction of the crowd was joyous but solemn. Attendees were keenly aware of the significance and the solemnity of the occasion.

This gesture of reconciliation on the part of the County Board of Supervisors, who had no connection to or relationship with members of the 1959 Board, has far reaching implications. Future generations, Black and White, will be reminded of this blot on race relations in the county. Hopefully, they will learn from this troubled history and move beyond it without forgetting it. This did not mean that henceforth race relations in the county would be perfect, that the shadow of slavery had been removed permanently from the Commonwealth. It did, however, signal a new beginning in race relations in the county.

The banquet attendees were told that the power of reconciliation is always "on time," as Christian faith reminds us—a fact underscored by Rev. Griffin's eldest son, Leslie Francis Griffin III, who was the keynote speaker at the banquet. In his speech, the young Mr. Griffin speculated what his father would have made of the commemoration on the lawn of the State Capitol in Richmond, the unveiling of the plaque on the lawn of the Prince Edward County courthouse, and the placing of the light of reconciliation in the cupola of the building. He suggested his father would probably be less interested in that and more interested in how Blacks were now faring in Prince Edward County and how many Black students were now enrolled at Longwood University.

As I witnessed the events taking place in Farmville that day, the flow of tears and the outpouring of emotions seemed to find no end. I had found the catharsis that I had naively hoped to find in the delivery of the persuasive speech to the members of my small speech class at my liberal arts college in Kentucky in 1965 but could not because the scar was more than superficial—it was a gaping wound! Now I know why the butterfly has come to take on symbolic meaning in my life. It is as if I had been in a bound state or cocoon both psychically and emotionally for fifty years, and this experience afforded me the opportunity to free myself from it, spread my wings, and move freely and with a lightness of a butterfly. Despite my personal metamorphosis ongoing since 1959, I am as clear-eyed as ever that racism has not disappeared from the fabric of the nation, for it is part parcel of its DNA. But I feel positive that on that day in Prince Edward County, a group of people made at least a small tear in that fabric and decided to move forward together, beginning a new day with renewed hope and confidence.

*Depiction of Barbara Johns leading the student strike at
the R. R.Moton High School on April 21, 1951.*

(Personal Collection)

Two of the panels of the Virginia Civil Rights monument unveiled on the Capitol grounds Monday, June 21, 2008.

(Personal Collection)

*The local Richmond newspaper estimated that about 4,000 people
attended the two-day event which culminated in the unveiling of
the Civil Rights monument. This photo shows some of the crowd.*

(Personal Collection)

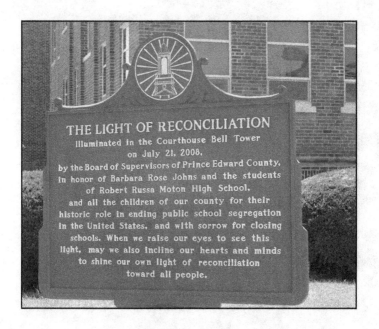

THE LIGHT OF RECONCILIATION
Illuminated in the Courthouse Bell Tower
on July 21, 2008,
by the Board of Supervisors of Prince Edward County,
in honor of Barbara Rose Johns and the students
of Robert Russa Moton High School,
and all the children of our county for their
historic role in ending public school segregation
in the United States, and with sorrow for closing
schools. When we raise our eyes to see this
light, may we also incline our hearts and minds
to shine our own light of reconciliation
toward all people.

The Board of Supervisors erected this plaque on the courthouse grounds admitting publicly that the actions taken by their predecessors fifty years earlier was morally wrong, and sincerely apologizing to the Black community for their actions.

(Personal Collection)

*The Light of Reconciliation ceremony took place on the front lawn
of the Prince Edward County courthouse in July 21, 2008.*

(Personal Collection)

The light of reconciliation as illuminated in the cupola of the Prince Edward County courthouse on that same evening in 2008.

(Personal Collection)

When I discover who I am,
I'll be free.

—*Ralph Ellison,* Invisible Man

I think you travel to search
And you come back to find yourself.

—*Nigerian writer Chimamandi Ngozi Adichie*

Each man's life represents a road toward himself.

—*German writer Hermann Hesse*

FOURTEEN

CODA: THE JOURNEY BACK

All journeys back are paradoxically journeys forward, for they connect present with past by unearthing memories and experiences that make us into the people we are today. They are matrices, if you will, onto which the threads of our lives and personhood are woven. Three journeys back to my past have been pivotal to my pulling together those major threads, of how I, Alfred Leon Cobbs, overcame the odds, persevered, achieved a great deal in life, and made my contribution to society, despite the fact that the odds seemed against me.

More than fifty years ago in 1959 when the lights

went out on public education in Prince Edward County, Virginia, my efforts to be the best student possible and make my contribution to society were thwarted. I had no idea what my future might hold or where it might lead. However, Providence guided me through my existential blindness during those years as I struggled to find my way out of the chaos which confronted me when public education was abolished.

In previous pages I have told the story of how I moved from a kid who literally "missed the bus" to one who received a complete formal education and became a professor of German at a major Midwestern university. Three commemorations marking the fiftieth anniversary of events affecting and shaping my path led me to an epiphany as to how the course of my life moved, how I found my way.

The first journey back was a return to South Hill, Virginia, in September 2013, to attend the commemoration of the sixtieth anniversary of the establishment of East End High School in 1953, one of two major high school facilities constructed for Blacks in Mecklenburg County, Virginia. When the schools in the county were desegregated in 1969, East End was first repurposed as the Park View Junior High School, serving grades eight and nine, and later as Park View Middle School, serving grades six through nine.

After receiving my diploma from East End in 1962, I returned a couple of times to a celebration of the school and its founding. This was when my host family, Mr. and Mrs. E. N. Taliaferro Sr., were still alive. Now I was returning again after more than fifty years. Once back in town it dawned on me that it had been a bit more than half a century since I had given the valedictory address, "Growth in Economic Power," which Mr. Taliaferro had helped me write, and had walked across the stage for the last time to receive my diploma.

Why was I returning after so many years? I had no real desire to participate because I felt no particular sense of belonging to the school or the community that supported it. The catalyst for my return was a phone call in April 2013 from the high school counselor for whom I had worked as a student assistant, Mr. Howard E. Robinson Sr., and his wife, Mrs. Anna S. Robinson, my homeroom teacher in the eleventh and twelfth grades and my twelfth-grade English teacher and senior sponsor. He was now in his early nineties and his wife in her mid-eighties. At their urging, and because of the possibility of seeing them again after more than forty years, with mixed emotions, I decided to send in my registration card to attend the celebration. According to the Robinsons, I needed to send it in early because of the possibility that people might be turned away if there was robust registration. I reasoned that if I decided not to go, I could cancel at the last minute or simply forego the reasonable registration and banquet fees.

As the date of the event approached, I still felt conflicted and seriously considered dropping out. As I examined what was happening on the gut level, I realized that I had some "unfinished business" with my East End High School and South Hill experience, one that had been thrust upon me by the Prince Edward County tragedy. On the one hand, there were the memories of the pain of separation from my parents and my two brothers at a time when we would have most desired to be together. On the other hand, there was the fear that I would feel like an outsider, an interloper, whom few, if any, of the students would remember after a half-century. Because I had no family connection in the area, I feared feeling like a stranger in a strange land.

The weekend consisted of a Friday afternoon picnic and a Saturday evening banquet. Because of my trepidation about the entire celebration, once I decided to go, I felt that I needed to attend the picnic in order to become reacquainted with a few people so that I would be able to sit among familiar faces at the banquet. After all, I had not kept in touch with anyone from the area, and the principal and his wife and their son with whom I had lived for three years were all deceased. At the picnic, which was held on a beautiful estate turned into a county recreation area, my misgiving slowly began to fade as I was received warmly by the hosts who did not know me at all. Then, the guests began arriving, and as soon as several of them saw my name tag, they recognized me right away; we began reminiscing about mutual past experiences and former teachers. It dawned on me in that moment that I had indeed been a part of and belonged to the high school community and my cohort group more than a half-century ago.

Over the many years that had passed since I received my high school diploma, I had forgotten that at least some of my classmates would surely remember me, for I had been junior class president, senior class vice president, class valedictorian, and one of the commencement speakers. Now I felt that I belonged to a "graduating class," something that I had never experienced at any of the Prince Edward County school celebrations. At this place and in this moment in time, I made a connection to my past that was sorely missing. I had taken another step in the process of healing the psychic wound that the Prince Edward County experience had caused me.

The rapport I established with my former classmates at the picnic led to my agreeing to sit with them at the

Saturday night banquet; they would save me a seat. About a dozen of my classmates from the class of 1962 attended and we did indeed sit together. The speaker for the occasion was Mrs. Lucille T. Hudson, who was supervisor of elementary education for Blacks in Mecklenburg County during the '50s and '60s. She was a woman in her nineties. In her talk she raised a series of questions about the history of the education of Blacks in the county as a way of engaging her audience. As she moved forward, she proceeded to supply the answers based on her knowledge of the history. She indicated that in 1871 there were 20 schools for Black students in the county, many of which were Rosenwald schools, supported by Julius Rosenwald, founder of Sears Roebuck and Co., or by the United Presbyterian Church. She cited Thyne Institute in Chase City as one of the examples. She went on to talk about the work of Mrs. Matilda Booker, who had a supervisory position in administering the schools, in furthering the educational opportunities for Blacks in the county. Finding no high school for Blacks in the eastern part of the county, Mrs. Booker worked tireless with community leaders, both Black and White, to establish the Mecklenburg Training School as a public high school in South Hill in the '20s. The successor to the MTS was East End High School, which opened in 1953. In the western end of the county West End High School (Clarksville) was opened in 1935.

With the desegregation of schools in the county, the Black high schools were repurposed as middle schools, and Black students were sent either to the Park View High School in the eastern part of the county or Bluestone High School in the western part of the county. In the course of her remarks, Mrs. Hudson spoke of the need for the Black community to find a way to preserve this history in some kind of repository for fear that it might otherwise be lost forever, given the fact that the schools in the county had now been desegregated for more than thirty years. She also indicated that in the early '50s, Attorney Oliver W. Hill from the NAACP state office had approached the Black community in Mecklenburg County about the possibility of Black parents being willing to sign a petition for the county to become one of the litigants in the *Brown v. Board of Education* suit. Since the parents were not willing to sign, the issue became a moot point. However, she mentioned that Prince Edward County had then become one of the litigants in the Supreme Court case; that at the time the schools were closed there in 1959, a student from Prince Edward had attended East End High School.

Practically as soon as Mrs. Hudson made her

statement, I raised my hand and could not resist saying "and he is here tonight." There was momentary silence in the room when I made the statement, and Mrs. Hudson's comments were, "You should be up here making the speech rather than me." At the end of the program there was an open mic period during which I thought I wanted to say something but hesitated until a former classmate, Marva Collins, urged me to get up and speak, and so I did. This was the first time that most of the people in the room had heard my story, for it was never revealed to them publicly at the time I attended East End, neither by the school leadership nor the local newspaper. Why? The school boards of counties adjoining or near Price Edward were leery of accepting students into their system without financial support. They also did not want to face the possibility of an influx of students that they could not accommodate. I observed all of the banquet attendees listening intently, and in that moment, felt an intimate connection with the community. And for the first time perhaps, I, and they as well, understood that our struggle has always been collective; that the categorizations of race and ethnicity in the American setting has placed us all "in the same boat."

The journey back to South Hill had not only been a physical one, one that was fifty years removed in time, but an existential one. I had left East End High School a bit more than a half century earlier still trying to find myself emotionally and spiritually, for I had missed the experience of my formative years growing up with my brothers and under the guidance of my parents and other adults in the Prince Edward County community.

As I drove the ninety miles along the quiet, scenic, and winding State Route 47 through the rolling hills of Central Virginia on that warm, beautiful, and sunny Sunday morning from South Hill to Pamplin, where I grew up and where some family members still lived, I reflected on, processed, and digested the experiences of the weekend. My psyche was flooded with rich memories and recollections of the East End High School and South Hill experiences of more than fifty years earlier. As I drove along, I began to see clearly that I did indeed belong to that community in the memories and experiences of those I met who had not forgotten me and my contributions.

The second journey back was to Prince Edward County in May 2014, to attend the local NAACP commemoration marking the anniversary of three landmark decisions that had a profound and life changing effect on the lives of the Black citizens of Prince Edward

County during the '50s and '60s. The events theme was "'Lest We Forget'—60 Years Since Brown." The three events commemorated were the sixtieth anniversary of *Davis v. County School Board of Prince Edward County*, one of the five litigants in the *Brown v. Board of Education* decision handed down in 1954 that overturned the *Plessy v. Ferguson* decision of 1896, upholding the doctrine of "separate but equal;" the fifty-fifth anniversary of the closing of public schools in 1959 rather than desegregate as the Supreme Court had ordered; and the fiftieth anniversary of the reopening of public schools in the county in 1964 as a result of the *Griffin v. County School Board of Prince Edward County* case of 1961.

One of the program events was a Saturday afternoon forum focused on how these three historical events affected the lives of those who were disadvantaged by the closing of the public schools in the county. During the open forum following the panel discussion, the question was asked: what kind of impact the Moton Museum, an institution whose establishment is rooted in Prince Edward County's 1951-1964 fight for educational equality for Black students, had on those directly affected by the closing of the schools from 1959-1964? When the question was raised, I had an introspective moment and felt an urge to respond. I began by saying that I initially felt that the Museum was not about my story, i.e., I did not feel a direct connection to it. After all, I had not graduated from high school in the county and felt no loyalty to a peer group with whom I had lost contact after the schools were closed, and I had no group of fellow graduates with whom I could identify.

As I began to talk about my emotions, memories of my return to South Hill, Virginia, in September 2013, began to swim back into my consciousness, I began to see that both experiences were fundamental in shaping who I have become. The Museum was indeed about my story! In hearing the panelists and the respondents in the open forum talk about how the Prince Edward County tragedy had impacted their lives in profound ways, I realized that all of our stories are threads in the tapestry that reflects the life experiences of those of us affected most profoundly by the tragedy of 1959. The Museum is indeed a historical repository of our memories and experiences, a reminder of our past, and a vehicle to continually tell our stories to future generations.

The third and final journey back was a return to Berea College, Kentucky, to the fiftieth anniversary celebration of the graduating class of 1966, which I attended with some trepidation. This experience is discussed in some detail in Chapter One and is the catalyst and the inspiration for my having decided to write my memoir. During the Berea College visit in 2016, I had conversations with a number of my White classmates about shared experiences inside and outside the classroom. Those of us who enrolled in German with one of the Kogermas reminisced about our experiences learning German; we talked about "Mountain Day" and the role it played in bonding among students and among students and faculty members; we talked about how all of us over the years learned to put into practice in our lives Berea's motto, "God has made of one blood all the peoples of the earth." And we marveled at how the Berea experience led to each of us having a success story that would not have been possible without it. Several of my classmates reminded me that my experience as a professor of German at a major Midwestern university was one of the great success stories of the Class of 1966. And I concur with that assessment.

The three journeys back to my past have helped me gather significant threads of my life into an existential tapestry, and I can now come to terms with the trauma of the Prince Edward County tragedy. In the process of writing my story, I have learned that the individual can triumph over adversity, *if* the conditions are favorable.

Often, the person facing the adversity is not in a position to challenge or change their circumstances without the direct help or intervention of others, who create the conditions under which the individual can "get a new lease on life" and find their way forward. In my case, the conditions were made favorable by the principal's family and the faculty of East End High School for me to reach my goal of finishing high school and receiving my diploma. They believed in me even when I was not sure that I believed in myself. With their help, I focused on my goal and devoted my energies to it until I received the prize. It provided me the foundation for further study and for taking the steps necessary to find a satisfying and fulfilling career. In the final analysis, mine is a story of the triumph of the human spirit in the face of what seemed at the time like insurmountable odds. As the line from the Negro spiritual, "Amazing Grace," attests, "I once was lost, but now am found. Was blind but now I see."

ACKNOWLEDGMENTS

Whenever one produces work of any kind, there are always a number of people to be thanked for the role that they have played in making the project possible. At the outset, I wish to thank my brothers, Samuel and Freddie, who were fellow sufferers in the struggle, for being there for me over the years as we all have found our way in life, and for sharing parts of their individual stories with me. I also want to thank countless family members and friends who have listened over the years to snippets of my story and suggested that it needed to be told. As well, I am grateful to the individuals who read drafts of the manuscript and gave me their feedback, among them, my sister, Patsy C. Franklin, my brothers, Samuel and Freddie, Freddie's wife Pattie, my niece, Cindy F. Saunders, and my good friends, Amanda Donigian of Detroit and Katharine and Madison Brown of Staunton, Virginia and Parkersburg, West Virginia.

While most of the pictures in the memoir are from my private collection, I wish to express my appreciation to the National Archives and Records Administration for the historical photos from the Moton and the Farmville High Schools at the time of the student strike. I am particularly indebted to Joni Albrecht for her able editorial assistance and her publishing "know how" in bringing this project to fruition. Finally, I wish to acknowledge the role that Lacy Ward Jr., Director of the Robert Russa Moton Museum from 2008-2014, played in establishing the contact between me and my very capable editor, without whose help the memoir may never have become a reality.

ABOUT THE AUTHOR

Alfred L. Cobbs grew up on a tobacco farm in the western end of Prince Edward County, Virginia, and attended the public schools in the county until they were closed in 1959 rather than desegregate, as ordered by the Supreme Court in the Brown v. Board of Education suit of 1954. From 1959-1962, he lived with a host family in Mecklenburg County, Virginia, where he graduated from the segregated local high school at the end of the three year period. After graduation he matriculated to Berea College, Kentucky, where he majored in German. Upon completion of his undergraduate education, he pursued graduate studies in German at the University of Missouri-Columbia and the University of Cincinnati, receiving his Ph.D. in 1974 from the Ohio institution. For nearly 50 years he taught German studies at three major institutions: University of Cincinnati, University of Virginia, and Wayne State University, where he spent the last 34 years of his career. He retired from Wayne State in 2013 and spends his retirement years doing international travel, volunteer work, and reading.